Under One Roof

SUNY Series in Urban Public Policy
James Bohland and Patricia Edwards, Editors

UNDER ONE ROOF

Issues and Innovations in Shared Housing

Edited by
George C. Hemmens,
Charles J. Hoch,
and Jana Carp

State University of New York Press

Published by
State University of New York Press, Albany

For information, address State University of New York
Press, State University Plaza, Albany, N.Y., 12246

The chapters in this book are based on papers first prepared and presented as lectures funded by the University Colloquium Series, Office of Housing Policy Research, Federal National Mortgage Association (Fannie Mae). Their support is gratefully acknowledged.

Production by Diane Ganeles
Marketing by Bernadette LaManna

Library of Congress Cataloging-in-Publication Data

Under one roof : issues and innovations in shared housing / edited by
George C. Hemmens, Charles J. Hoch, and Jana Carp.
  p.   cm. — (SUNY series in urban public policy)
  Includes bibliographical references and index.
  ISBN 0-7914-2905-9 (ch : alk. paper). — ISBN 0-7914-2906-7 (pb :
alk. paper)
  1. Shared housing—United States. 2. Shared housing—Government
policy—United States. 3. Poor—Housing—Government policy—United
States. 4. Aged—Housing—Government policy—United States.
6. Housing policy—United States. I. Hemmens, George C. II. Hoch,
Charles, 1948– . III. Carp, Jana. IV. Series.
HD7287.86.U6U53   1996
363.5—dc20   95-18576
                                                           CIP

Contents

Tables

Figures

CHAPTER 1

Introduction

Shared housing arrangements provide an important complement to conventional housing options for all segments of the population. Defined broadly, shared housing combines common facilities for joint use and shared responsibility for governing this use. Housing providers sell single family dwellings and town homes in condominium and planned unit developments that use formalized sharing to enhance access to home ownership. Thus, for millions of middle-class households, shared housing masquerades as independent home ownership. In contrast, current policy and public opinion oppose efforts to justify and support shared housing for the poor or those people whose needs appear marginal and undeserving from the viewpoint of middle-income buyers anxious to protect their own vulnerability. But this prejudice against the poor, the disabled, the single parent family, and other vulnerable households remains hidden behind the selective use of development regulations supported by the myth that the single family house, designed exclusively for the nuclear family, offers the ideal home for everyone. These chapters expose the unfair practices and policies this myth supports, and so encourage efforts to treat fairly people living in all forms of shared housing, while providing arguments, evidence, and stories to document the value and legitimacy of informal sharing.

Residential structures can be designed to accommodate sharing for members of different social classes, whether transitional housing for the homeless or co-housing for the middle-class. Sharing itself does not impose the stigma of dependency or low status, at least not if undertaken free of moral and legal sanction from outside. Many households and community organizations currently modify the structure and use of the physical housing stock to meet a diverse assortment of social needs. Nationally, thousands of individual owners use informal and frequently illegal means to convert housing to shared use. Nonprofit organizations construct shared housing for special populations whose age, abilities or illness make conventional housing arrangements obsolete or even dangerous. These innovations in shared housing persist despite regulations that restrict or

1

banish shared residences for the poor and needy from single-family zoned neighborhoods including shared single-family type homes, elder cottages, and accessory apartments. We conclude that people and government should treat all forms of sharing equally instead of privleging sharing for those with economic advantages. Removing the stigma paves the way for reforming overly restrictive regulations and policies.

Sharing and the Single Family Dwelling

Ownership of the single family dwelling has for the past fifty years signified social and economic success for all but the poorest households in the United States. First, government and the building industry worked hard to make ownership economically affordable, socially attractive, and politically desirable. Second, increasing real incomes for the vast majority of the population meant that more households could purchase the space and privacy of single-family dwellings, usually in the suburbs. The one-two combination of prosperity and subsidy paid off. After World War II single-family housing starts shot up from 114,000 in 1944 to 1,692,000 in 1950 (Jackson 1985: 233). The proportion of households who owned their home increased from a century low of 43.6 percent in 1940 to a peak of 64.4 percent in 1980 (Devaney 1994: 21). Accompanying and fueling this shift, the nuclear household, living in its own single-family home, was promoted and celebrated as the desirable social norm, a norm that increasingly rings hollow as economic middle-class prosperity fades and households change shape.

Industry and government have maintained support for home owner-ship even though the real income for most households has leveled off or declined over the past twenty years. Unable to enter the homeowner market, many newly forming moderate and middle income households have been forced to remain in a rental market that has little government support and usually receives general public contempt. As this demand for rental housing has increased, so have rents (Apgar 1990: 31–32).

Large developers anticipated this affordability problem during the 1960s by adopting the use of the common interest development (CID). Conventional subdivision procedures treat each lot and house as an independent product. The purchaser pays for shared facilities and utilities as part of the purchase price or through local taxes. But the rising costs for conventional subdivision in the 1960s and 1970s encouraged developers to find ways to increase development density and decrease the cost of residential infrastructure. In the common interest development (usually either a condominium or planned unit development), purchasers join a private nonprofit homeowners' association established by the developer that regulates property use for the entire development. CIDs enable developers to cluster housing units on less space, reduce infrastructure expense, and offer formerly individual amenities (e.g., swimming pools) as shared amenities. This version of shared housing for the middle-class proved astonishingly popular. There were barely 200 common interest developments in the United States in 1960. But by 1993 the number of homeowners associations had skyrocketed to 150,000—housing some 32 million people in more than 12 million housing units. This is out of a national housing stock of 102 million units (Community Associations Institute 1993).

Contemporary residents rarely grasp the social and political implications of their shared membership in homeowner associations. Responsibilities that first appear as fine print in the deed do not register for buyers eager to purchase their own home, such as landscaping requirements, color codes, and other restrictive covenants. Residents usually discover much later that association rules prohibit the use of their property in unexpected ways. Submitting to the shared rules of private covenants protects the economic and social value of each house as it reduces the individual autonomy of each owner (McKenzie 1994).

Ironically to our point of view, CIDs perpetuate the myth of the single family dwelling and its autonomous inhabitants rather than promote community social life among the diverse households that live there. The shared covenants restrict the appearance and use of the property regardless of household composition and need. The homeowner associations buttress beliefs about the virtue of home ownership for the nuclear family, even as declining housing affordability, increasing household variety and changing social values challenge the relevance and workability of this housing option for everyone.[1]

Housing Needs that Challenge the American Dream

The desire for a high degree of privacy and autonomy in the choice of a residence shapes the public conception of "good" housing for all segments of the population. Many public policies, like zoning laws, subsidize and promote the development of single-family homes while outlawing or at best ignoring shared housing accommodations. The private detached dwelling inhabited by a nuclear family, however, has only just recently become the predominant form of residential housing in the United States. The rapid growth of American cities in the late nineteenth and early twentieth century encouraged the construction of high density apartments and apartment hotels for families, and boarding, rooming and lodging house accommodations for single adults, most of whom were recent urban migrants. Apartment hotels offered an attractive and fashionable option for prosperous middle-class families, while rooming houses sheltered mobile middle-class singles. For instance, Chicago possessed 2,424 rooming houses in 1915, a number that had increased almost fivefold during the previous 30 years. One near North Side neighborhood housed 23,007 roomers, while Chicago's skid row lodging houses sheltered somewhere between 40,000 and 60,000 single poor people (Hoch and Slayton 1989: 16, 92). The development and promotion of high density urban hotels and rooming houses waned from the 1920s onward as professional reformers, real estate developers, and federal officials promoted ownership of suburban single-family dwellings at the expense of the variety of dense city housing forms.

Paul Groth, in a recent historical review of attitudes toward hotel living, describes vividly how the promotion of the one family–one house ideal came at the expense of other forms of residential life. He quotes Lawrence Veiller, a leader in housing reform writing in 1905, "The bad effect on the community of a congregate form of living is by no means limited to poor people. Waldorf-Astorias at one end of town and 'big flats' at the other are equally bad in their destruction of civic spirit and the responsibilities of citizenship." In 1903 the Architectural Record complained that communal dining was the "consummate flower of domestic irresponsibility,... the sacrifice of everything implied by the word 'home'." Even the University of Chicago sociologist, Ernest Burgess, writing in 1926 after extensive fieldwork, could still say that "the small family group in apartment houses and hotels" was "The most notorious illustration of effectual detachment from the claims of kinship" (Groth 1994: 201, 210).

Declining Prosperity and Changing Households

As long as the availability and affordability of purchasing single-family suburban dwellings was high, the free standing single-family dwelling on a parcel of land allowing setbacks all around appeared compelling as a social objective for those who wanted to pursue this way of life. Since 1973, economic constraints have hampered household formation and successful home purchase by young moderate and middle-income individuals. In addition, the number and kind of households has increased in response to marital breakups, life cycle changes, and changing social mores. The proportion of unmarried couples living together has increased, as has the share of empty nest households. Most striking is the increase in female-headed households with children. It was mainly due to lack of means, but among scattered minorities the desire for other housing forms was growing (See Table 1).

TABLE 1

Households by Type, U.S. Total: 1940 to 1990

	Number in Millions		Percent Change
Characteristic	1940	1990	1940–90
Total Households	34.9	91.9	163%
Family Householder	31.5	64.5	105
Married Couples	26.6	50.7	91
Male, No Wife	1.5	3.1	108
Female, No Husband	3.4	10.7	213
Nonfamily Householder	3.5	27.4	693
Male	1.6	12.1	659
Female	1.9	15.3	722

Source: (Devaney 1994: 16)

The future availability and access to the suburban single-family home relies on a convergence of economic, social, and political forces that no longer flow with the same strength or in parallel. Efforts are underway to revive and rechannel the diverging streams along the same route. In addition to the widespread use of CIDs, builders offer downsized versions of the single-family dwelling with more or fewer amenities. The Federal National Mortgage Association (FNMAE) offers subsidy schemes to reduce downpayment requirements for first time homebuyers hoping to increase demand for single-family mortgages. Local governments develop increasingly sophisticated land use restrictions to protect against the threat of eroding property values and to police illegal conversions in middle-class neighborhoods. These efforts intend to maintain existing development patterns that privilege single-family housing development.

The Growing Ranks of the Poor

Providing housing for the poor has long been a central focus of government housing policy in most industrially-developed countries. The quality and scope of programs vary enormously from country to country, but significant institutional innovations have led to more and better housing for the poor than had been offered previously. In the United States, for instance, early housing reformers at the turn of the century deplored the wretched living conditions for the poor inhabitants of the slums, and many of their proposals to eliminate the slums and replace the tenements with higher standard accommodations have been implemented. The widespread destruction of the substandard housing stock, especially in the urban slums, increased the quality of the housing stock nationwide. As long as the growth in the real income of the poor (whether by subsidy or wages) kept pace with such improvements, a growing portion of the poor enjoyed improved housing conditions. This achievement was announced by the analysts of the Housing Commission Report prepared for the Reagan administration in 1981. The United States had solved the housing quality problem, but not the housing affordability problem.

Despite numerous government efforts to increase the income of the poor, the 1990s finds the scope and intensity of shelter poverty increasing in the United States and other industrial countries. Changing patterns of economic growth and decline have shifted greater burdens of economic uncertainty onto the poor. Real income for the poor has declined precipitously over the past decade. As the poor get poorer, fewer can afford to remain in, or even enter, the bottom of the housing market. The supply of low rent housing has not kept pace with rising demand in some areas, and the supply has contracted in others. Homelessness emerges, less a temporary problem than a chronic condition.[2]

Members squeezed out of the shrinking middle-class and others joining the growing underclass, especially young adults, face affordability gaps that put owning a single-family dwelling out of reach. Economic necessity forces many to live with kin or friends much longer than they would like. Those unable or unwilling to buy into a CID face the combination of disappointed expectations and enforced doubling up that can make residential sharing a source of shame rather than an opportunity to economize and even build community.

The chapters in this book offer argument and evidence that challenge our exclusive attachment to the single (nuclear) family dwelling and our corresponding neglect of shared housing arrangements for the numerous households that do not fit the prototype of the nuclear family. When residents voluntarily collaborate in the design, management, and use of shared accommodations, they can overcome the indignity of necessity in modest yet meaningful ways. Shared housing arrangements provide an important complement to conventional housing options.

Households and community organizations do currently modify the structure and use of the physical housing stock to meet a diverse assortment of social needs. Middle-class families collaborate to produce cohousing arrangements that provide space for group meals and play, while ensuring private living quarters for each family. Nonprofit organizations construct housing designed to meet the social and physical needs of special populations whose age, disabilities, or illness make conventional housing arrangements obsolete or even dangerous. Households take in kin or friends suffering social and economic hardship.

Unlike the impersonal reciprocity in legal and monetary exchanges that define traditional housing arrangements (e.g., the lease and the mortgage) and the more recent CIDs, shared housing requires reciprocity and participation among residents as each learns what to expect and how to contribute to the domestic welfare of the entire household. Residents of shared housing do not only agree to a contract, but enter a domestic community in which they agree to participate.

We often imagine such communities using ideological concepts that polarize and exaggerate the difference between community and individuality. In ideological debates joining a community requires sacrificing individuality, while obtaining independence demands sundering all ties of community dependence. Housing policy and development practices have tended in this century to emphasize and foster images of household independence that ignore and occasionally deny the importance of social community in residential life. Shared housing appears quaint, weird, threatening, or otherwise exceptional because of the now widespread belief in the desirability and value of the single-family home. However, challenging the belief on ideological grounds is foolish, since the advantages of home ownership for individual households remain obvious, even if a diminishing possibility. The problem is not individual home ownership for nuclear families, but the system of ideological, legal, and cultural beliefs that enshrine this housing option as the only "good" housing to the detriment of alternative housing that better meets many people's needs and wants.

Defining Shared Housing

The definition of shared housing reflects different conceptions of what and how residents share, whether dwelling, social life, tenure or rent. Each of these kinds sharing may be used to classify one type of shared housing (e.g., roommates), but frequently the relationships are more complex. For instance, a boarding house resident is likely to rent a private room while using a bath, kitchen, or other space in common. Residents are most likely to rely on the landlord manager or caretaker for the maintenance of common spaces. In-kind rent arrangements for the care of common spaces (e.g., cleaning living room and hallways) are usually considered desirable, but are not frequent in practice. Yet in all these instances, sharing refers to an intentional and purposeful commitment by participating households. Prisons, military barracks and emergency shelters in which members involuntarily share common facilities, therefore, do not count as shared housing.

Figure 1 provides a scheme for classifying different types of shared housing that currently exist by combining what people share: physical dwelling, social life, tenure, and rent. The types listed in the first column of the figure are clustered by sponsorship category: shared ownership, private ownership, and institutional ownership. Shared ownership applies to shared housing arrangements in which residents possess legal ownership rights to use and obligations to care for the common space. Common interest developments (condominiums, cooperatives, and planned unit developments) offer the most prominent example of these arrangements. Mingles refer to a kind of condominium arrangement where two unattached adults purchase a unit with two or more bedrooms but only one kitchen and bath. Private ownership includes shared housing units purchased through mortgage agreements and rented to tenants with lease agreements. Nonprofit ownership includes shared housing units purchased, financed, and managed by a nonprofit agency for the benefit of shared housing residents. Rows in Figure 1 include the most frequently mentioned types of shared housing. The responses in the cells of the figure denote what particular kinds of sharing are most likely to occur in each type of shared housing.

FIGURE 1

Kinds of Shared Housing by Sponsorship and Type of Sharing

	Physical Sharing			Social Sharing			Tenure		Rent Sharing		
	Room	Bath/Kitchen	Common Space	Sociability	Reciprocity	Caretaking	Ownership	Rental	Rental Mortgage	In-kind	Subsidy
SHARED											
Collective		Yes	Yes	Yes	Yes	Yes	Yes		Yes	Yes	
Coop			Yes	Yes	Yes		Yes		Yes	Some	
Mingles	Yes	Yes	Yes	Yes	Some		Yes		Yes		
Condo			Yes	Some			Yes		Yes		
PRIVATE											
Boarding		Yes	Yes	Yes	Yes	Yes		Yes	Yes	Some	
Rooming		Yes	Some	Yes	Some			Yes	Yes	Some	
SRO		Yes	Yes	Yes	Yes			Yes	Yes		
Echo			Yes	Yes	Some	Some	Some	Yes	Yes	Some	
Accessory			Yes	Yes	Yes	Some	Some	Yes	Yes	Some	
INSTITUTIONAL											
Congregate			Yes	Some	Some	Some	Yes		Yes		Some
Transitional	Some	Yes	Yes	Yes	Some	Yes		Yes		Some	Yes
Women Shltr	Some	Yes	Yes	Yes	Some	Yes		Yes		Some	Yes
Group Homes	Some	Yes	Yes	Yes	Some	Yes		Yes		Some	Yes

Note: Yes means sharing very likely.
      A blank space means sharing unlikely.
      Some means occassional sharing.

Physical Sharing

Physical sharing occurs when multiple households inhabit the same residential site or structure, and at least two households use the same bath, kitchen, and/or other space in common, in addition to the entrance. The structure may be small—a two-bedroom house in which the owner uses one bedroom and rents the other room to a tenant who shares the kitchen, bath, and other rooms. Shared housing accommodations may also be large—a 200 unit SRO hotel whose residents use bath facilities and other services in common or a large congregate housing project for the elderly.

All forms of shared housing allow for individual possession and control of some private space. At one extreme are institutional facilities for the poor, such as transitional shelters and SRO hotels. Although shelter providers usually offer private sleeping rooms for resident households, limited budgets and increased demand require that sleeping rooms be shared by several households. When a residential facility can no longer provide private space for individual households and these households must share all the spaces in which they live, sharing loses its voluntary character and becomes an imposition. At the other extreme are CIDs and cohousing arrangements, in which middle-class households each possess complete dwelling units, while sharing a common garden, laundry, dining room, workshop, or other facilities on a carefully landscaped site.

Social Sharing

Social sharing occurs when at least two households living in the same structure take joint responsibility for their use of some space in common. Each household respects the use of common spaces by others so as to ensure their own access and use of such spaces. Adopting and following customary practices of propriety, cleanliness, and security establishes a minimal reciprocity that enables households to share the same facilities based on the relatively thin social bonds of neighborliness or sociability, without requiring residents to take on the deeper responsibilities of friendship or kin.

Responsibility for joint use may also rely on the more substantial social bonds of mutual obligation and/or shared dependency. People may voluntarily choose to form a residential collective in which they not only share common space, but common values and obligations with each other. In these collectives, the households define themselves as members of a residential community rather than individual private households who simply share common facilities (e.g., fraternities, convents, communes). The responsibility of shared use may not always rest exclusively with residents. CID residents who do not want the hassle of maintaining a pool or golf course or residents whose reason for living together is based on conditions of shared vulnerability and dependency, for instance, dependent elderly, teenaged single mothers, homeless families, and others, may not be willing or able to care adequately for the common spaces each uses. Responsibility for the use of common spaces is then managed by caretakers who may negotiate with residents a variety of agreements for the joint care of common spaces.

Tenure

Shared tenure takes two forms: resident or absentee ownership. Resident owners share their dwelling with co-owners or tenants, while absentee owners rent their dwelling to tenants who share the use of common space. When the owner or co-owners share the same dwelling with tenants, the owners tend to care for and manage the housing as home rather than as just a business venture. Disinvestment or deferred maintenance is highly unlikely as it would come at the expense of the owners' standard of living. Usually, these arrangements are of a much smaller scale than shared housing accommodations managed by absentee owners.

Absentee ownership offers the opportunity to operate shared housing arrangements as a profit making business or a nonprofit housing resource for low income households. The combination of small residential quarters, high density, and shared common spaces can produce efficient, affordable housing without abandoning privacy for individual tenants.

Rent Sharing

Virtually all shared housing arrangements require payment of rent. In many, especially those in which deep social ties are present, needy tenants may substitute in-kind services for cash rent. Some cohousing arrangements will adjust mortgage payments and condominium association fees based on household income. Shared housing arrangements sponsored by government agencies or nonprofit organizations will frequently subsidize the rents of poor tenants in shared housing arrangements (e.g., congregate housing for the elderly) or perhaps subsidize the financing and construction of the shared housing units in order to keep rents below market rates. An example of this is using McKinney Act funds to rehabilitate SRO hotels as housing for homeless individuals.

Benefits of Sharing

The provision of shared housing options offers a promising alternative to meet the increasing demand for affordable, decent, and secure housing and offers benefits both to the individuals and households who share and to the larger community.

Sharing common facilities among several residents reduces the rent burden of each. For instance, an elderly homeowner receives rent from the homesharing tenant to offset mortgage and property tax expenses, while the tenant may enjoy a rent significantly below market rates for studio and one bedroom apartments. Shared housing can also make amenities and services available to residents that they could not otherwise afford. For example, a homesharing resident may enjoy access to a living room, garden, or common space not available if renting a studio or apartment. Similarly, residents can receive valuable services from each other in the form of shared meal preparation, personal chores, building maintenance, and household repairs. Sharing also offers each resident the opportunity to rely on the availability of others to meet particular social and personal needs, while meeting the specific needs of others in return.

Homesharing increases the availability of affordable housing stock in a relatively inexpensive fashion. Providing for more, smaller, private units in shared housing arrangements not only makes for greater affordability (less private space, less rent), but also accommodates the increasing number of single-person households. Homesharing increases neighborhood and community stability by enabling both senior and younger residents with relatively less income than the more prosperous middle-age cohort to stay in their home neighborhoods. In older communities this helps ensure the social continuity and diversity of the neighborhood. As a result, public facilities remain in use which might otherwise have been abandoned well before becoming obsolete (e.g., schools, neighborhood parks). Homesharing puts the aging housing stock to a more efficient use. When two or more people, formerly living in separate dwellings, share one large dwelling it releases the dwellings they left for others to purchase or rent. Shared housing offers affordable housing without costly public subsidies, while providing an alternative to apartment complexes.

The Stigma of Shared Housing

The conventional ideal of the single-family dwelling diminishes the social meaning and practical value of shared accommodations. So too does the belief about the moral influence of home ownership that links possession of a single-family home with ideals of self-reliance. The homeowner appears a better citizen than the renter. This belief not only binds individual virtue with exclusive possession of a home, but inspires institutional policies that favor individual home ownership over other forms of housing tenancy. For several generations Americans have learned to accept shared tenancy if done out of necessity rather than voluntary choice: for example, the college student who shares an apartment with others to cut costs, the adult child living at home to save funds for purchase of her own home, or the poor immigrants doubling up to reduce rent and save income for other needs. In all these cases, sharing appears acceptable because it is an involuntary and temporary accommodation to necessity, rather than a long term residential living arrangement. Presumably, then, if involuntary necessity and disciplined group life characterize shared tenancy, then sharing must reduce individual freedom and privacy.

The stigma of residential sharing flows not only from this presumption of involuntary necessity, but also from association with other forms of group quarters such as dormitories, barracks, jails, prisons, halfway houses, group homes, shelters, and nursing homes in which institutional caretakers and rules organize residential sharing. Most homeowners look with suspicion on the placement of such facilities nearby as a threat to property values and a source of social contagion.

The models of the housing market and the practice of real estate sales reproduce this housing status hierarchy with the single-family dwelling at the top, and group quarters of all sorts at the bottom. Existing zoning regulations mirror and reinforce the hierarchy by enforcing geographically homogeneous clusters of housing, while decades of investment in massive numbers of single-family units carries with it a powerful incentive to continue.

We do not expect people to abandon the single-family house. Possession and use of single-family housing units offers a wide assortment of valuable benefits for most households. However, we believe that claims about the superior moral and social value of exclusive possession and use of a house ignore the diverse needs of changing households, while justifying unnecessary social, legal, and political barriers to the development of shared housing alternatives.

Overview of Book

The chapters that follow answer the following questions: How do the benefits of reciprocity in shared housing compare in relationship to the loss of autonomy among the poor? How much of the housing stock has been physically converted to allow for shared living? What do buildings designed for shared living look like? How do they function? How do shared accommodations work for middle-class families as well as poor singles and the retired elderly? How should we respond to the increasing numbers of women and men earning their livings in homes designed to exclude work related activity? What role does local government play in controlling shared housing? A brief summary of each chapter follows.

Hemmens and Hoch draw on ten years of research with low income white and minority households in particular Chicago neighborhoods to describe routine house-sharing arrangements. Many residents, especially homeowners, provide shelter for relatives and friends coping with economic and personal problems. Home sharing arrangements can include a variety of households, most of whose members help manage, maintain, and support the house. Home sharing is an important part of a larger pattern of informal help among these households. Unable to access and afford the autonomy of middle-class residential choice, households offer a variety of shared housing arrangements instead. It is not too surprising then that residents consider the willingness to share as an important sign of positive moral character.

The poor double-up during recessions, but this requires owners who will subdivide and convert units to meet demand. These conversions are mainly illegal additions, violating the strict zoning and building codes designed to maintain the residential hierarchy. Anna Hardman uses national statistics from the American Housing Survey to identify additions to the housing stock due to conversion activity. Reviewing case study research on owners who convert their buildings, Hardman finds that neighborhood response to conversion activity varied with the attributes of the stock and the characteristics of the landlord. Local research findings suggest that positive additions to the housing stock may be made by simultaneously reducing regulatory restrictions, encouraging informal additions to housing stock, strengthening tenant rights, and supporting small property owners.

In her essay on shared housing, Sherry Ahrentzen describes the relationship between physical design and social reciprocity in predominantly middle-class co-housing arrangements and transitional shelters for the homeless poor. Residential structures can be designed to accommodate sharing for members of different social classes, whether transitional housing for the homeless or co-housing for the middle-class. Sharing does not itself impose the stigma of dependency or low status, at least not if undertaken free of moral and legal sanction from outside. Ahrentzen offers numerous examples of designs for shared housing and the interaction of design and social structure in the United States and Europe to show how design can enhance housing options by providing a balance between private and public shared space.

Jean Butzen describes how one Chicago non-profit corporation has developed a brand of single-room occupancy housing that fosters community as it strives for affordability. She describes how the organization combines the financing and acquisition of buildings, property management, provision of social service programs, and community interaction called "blended management". Instead of separating the physical and the social, the staff together with residents share responsibility for property management and social service programs on a daily basis. Residents enjoy the privacy of their small rooms, while having direct access to a variety of social supports and common facilities.

Nursing homes offer an increasingly unacceptable solution to the shelter needs of an aging population. Yet despite near universal misgivings about the desirability of nursing home care, most Americans lack residential alternatives between independent living and total care. Richard Biddlecombe describes how Abbeyfield International offers a variety of shared housing arrangements to fill this gap. Abbeyfield's 1100 independent houses are the product of the joint effort of local nonprofit developers, staff, and residents. Abbeyfield houses emphasize a cooperative spirit and a 'family' atmosphere. The design and management of different homes reflect differences in residents' need for balance between independence and support, while providing them both privacy and companionship for residents.

Jacqueline Leavitt briefly explores how economic restructuring and changing social relations have affected the location and nature of women's work, with particular impacts depending on race and ethnicity. The contemporary trend of home-based work (such as telecommuting) as a substitute for labor market participation outside the home, requires homeworking women to structure their residences and time to accommodate work. Architectural design can enable shared residences for various income levels to successfully combine home with work. At Nickerson Gardens, a public housing project in Los Angeles, unemployed residents use home space to participate in the informal economy, and activists encourage service-oriented home-based work as job creation and as community development. The opportunity for home-based work for otherwise unemployed residents in public housing projects has implications for the design and retro-fitting of low-income shared housing.

The social barriers to shared housing find legal support in local land use controls, according to housing analyst Patricia Pollak. Single-family zoning, created in part to perpetuate the single-family house, promotes a way of life that the majority of the population in the United States no longer lives. Pollak argues that zoning regulations greatly restrict or banish shared residences from single-family zoned neighborhoods, including shared single-family type homes, elder cottages, and accessory apartments. Although challenges to the legality of zoning classification have focused especially on the restrictive definition of family, Pollak concludes that issues of land use and density will play a decisive role in determining which forms of shared housing eventually receive legal approval.

Sharing contrasts dramatically with the formal and impersonal relationships of legal contract and economic exchange. But even as we doubt the mythical and rhetorical link between the virtues of home ownership and community improvement, we must beware embracing the opposite belief in reciprocal sharing as the exclusive source of community renewal. Peter Marris offers some useful cautions, arguing that sharing, rather than being a spontaneous or easily managed relationship, requires trust and predictability in everyday behavior, mutual agreement, and effective sanctions against unreliability. Despite our attachment to individual autonomy, most of us live most of our lives sharing housing with others, usually family members. Marris observes that such sharing arrangements are actually "sharing out"—for example, taking turns cooking meals, or using private bedrooms. What cannot be so easily shared out (the use of bathrooms or the television) becomes a focus of conflict and negotiation. Sharing between people who are not part of the same family or household raises the same issues of how mutual obligations and privacy can be balanced and protected.

These chapters give reason to reconsider conventional assumptions about the undesirability and marginality of shared accommodations. Shared housing has drawbacks, but does offer an efficient, decent, and relatively unstudied form of housing for many kinds of households. We need to pay careful attention to how changing households are adapting the existing housing stock to meet their needs and what can be done to help them put this stock to better use. Since family, social, and cultural relationships play the central role in determining the value of this housing rather than the market, shared housing arrangements get lumped into a residual category.

Local, state, and federal efforts to protect, enhance, and promote individual home ownership have gone too far. The obsession with the American Dream house has not only failed to address the diversity of need and desire for other forms of residential accommodation, but outlawed them. There are large portions of the population for whom individual home ownership and occupancy is unaffordable, undesirable, or both. These include large portions of the poor, but also more prosperous households who want to work at home, nurture a residential community, or cope with the vulnerabilities of illness or aging by living with others. Our purpose is simple, if difficult. We hope these readings will persuade readers that sharing offers a legitimate and useful residential housing option for many of these households in the United States, regardless of social class, gender, or race.

Notes

1. The social costs of middle-class CIDs are only now starting to obtain widespread public recognition (Barton and Silverman 1994; McKenzie 1994).

2. The literature counting, describing, and analyzing the homeless has expanded exponentially over the past decade. See for instance: Baum and Burnes 1993; Burt 1992; Dear and Wolch 1993; Ringheim 1990; Rossi 1989; Wright 1989.

CHAPTER 2

Shared Housing in Low Income Households

George Hemmens and Charles Hoch

The common perception is that people do not share housing except in extraordinary circumstances. This chapter questions the conventional view through an examination of the housing experience of low income families in several Chicago neighborhoods. We will argue that for these households home, the residential household of persons living together on a daily basis, is a principal source of support. This is where they get help and where they give it. These households, through sharing space and providing free housing units, use their housing as an asset. Households change composition, and household membership changes, as others are permitted to move in and out of the household in response to personal and economic changes. Thus household membership becomes help for those in need, and the home itself is often the most important resource people have for helping others. For these households, house sharing occurs in a larger framework of informal helping—the sharing of goods, services, advice, and support—which is an important part of their daily lives.

The information on the housing use of the Chicago households reported on in this chapter is extracted from an extended research project on the effects of the 1980s recession on low income families. The study focused on the households' use of public agency services and the sharing of informal help with relatives, friends, and neighbors as they coped with daily living. The households were selected from three low income neighborhoods where people appeared to be self-sufficient at the onset of the recession; these areas are not the poorest in the City. East Side is a predominantly white, working-class area on Chicago's southeast side. South Austin is a predominantly African-American community on the western edge of Chicago. Little Village is a predominantly Hispanic community several miles southwest of downtown Chicago. Eighty-nine households were originally interviewed in 1983 and again in 1985. Some of the households were interviewed again in 1987 and in 1992.

The reality and complexity of house sharing is most clearly presented in these households' own descriptions. So we open with some of their stories to illustrate different ways housing is shared. We then discuss patterns of house sharing, household change, and informal helping revealed through our interviews. Finally we turn to the question of motivation for sharing and the relation of house sharing to a more general practice of informal helping.

House Sharing

East Side

Like many people in East Side, Louise and Alvin Rudder lived in the community all their lives. It is an area characterized by family ties and life centered around the extended family and other community institutions, especially church and private social clubs. The area was settled by immigrants from central and eastern Europe, and that ethnic origin is still prominent in the community, although the community is now home to an increasing number of Hispanic households. In the conversation that follows, Louise, then 73, talks about her house.

> My daughter lives across the street from me, which I am very happy about. It is her daughter (and husband) that lives over me. Now she is married, and she has her new profession. She is a music therapist for which I am real happy. But she has MS and once in a while she is affected with it. She has been doing fairly good and now she is happy in her job. They do all the shoveling of the snow. They cut the grass which is a big help. Of course we return by not charging a lot of rent, you know. But you do have to charge something. Of course, she is a sweet person anyway. She always likes to say: 'Grams do you want something from the store?' or 'Can I do something?' Her husband is a taxidermist. He does it as a hobby. He is a draftsman at his work. We have furnished him with a room that used to be our old oil drum room. With my daughter living across the street it's real lovely. She does a lot of things for me. She works too.

Typically, the other apartment in the family's two-flat is not rented on the open market, but used as a resource for supporting family. Louise describes the history of this upstairs apartment where her granddaughter now lives.

> I first had my son there, then I had my daughter, then I had my niece, then I had my best girlfriend. I had one real dear girlfriend that we were

like this ever since we were in kindergarten. We had his [her husband's] cousin; she was up there. Well after a time that she lived up there, her husband passed away and now she is in a home. She lost her sight. So I go to visit her about once a month, to keep in touch with her because she was so used to being with us, for about twelve years. She knew all the family, you know. She was born herself, only across the street.

And she talks about the house.

I think my husband was born here, in this house and he is going to be eighty. Of course, he comes from a family of twelve. So that is why the house is quite as big as it is. When we took it over, after the parents died, we added this back room. We thought if things got bad, because we came up during the depression days, why if things got bad, we could always break it in half and have two apartments here. I lived across the street in the house my daughter lives in. That is where I was raised. I used to tell the kids, when we went together, when he was courting me, he didn't have to go around the block. People were real neighborly. You knew their mother and father, sisters and brothers and that.

For a hundred years these two houses across the street from each other have sheltered and supported this family. Louise and Alvin first lived in her parents' house, later took over that house after her parents' death, and eventually moved into his parents' house. This stability is not unusual for this neighborhood, or for other ethnic, working class neighborhoods in Chicago and other cities. The nearby steel mills and related industries provided good employment opportunities for many years, and young men in the neighborhood typically followed their fathers into the mills. Louise and Alvin's brothers and sisters left the neighborhood, while they stayed behind using the parental home as their residence and a base for the extended family carrying on family traditions and maintaining community institutions.

With the decline and closing of local industries over the last two decades, the opportunity to continue the old community lifestyle diminished. Young families like the Walshs, however, shared housing to cope with economic hardship. In 1985 Alice was 25 and her husband, Bob, was 27. They had two boys, 4 and 2. When first married, Alice and Bob lived in the basement of her parents' two-story brick home. They later moved into the small two bedroom apartment on the second floor of a frame house at the back of her parents' lot. Typical of rental patterns in the neighborhood, Alice's cousin had rented the apartment before her. The downstairs apartment in the back house has been rented for many years to an elderly man from the community.

The help with housing was essential for the Walshs. First, it gave them the opportunity to save money and start their family early in their marriage. Second, it sustained them through hard times. In 1985, Bob had been on strike for four years from the industrial job he held in the area. He had held another, lower paying job for the last two years, while still supporting the strike and hoping to see it resolved. During the two years he was unemployed, they did not use public assistance. As Alice tells it, "He got unemployment for a while, and I worked for a while, and we had our savings. Before we got married, we both worked and saved some money, so we didn't really have to go get food stamps or anything like that." They were able to get by without institutional help in part because they could live in her parents' apartment.

In both the Rudder and the Walsh house, the number of separate dwelling units fluctuates. No one lives in Alice's parents' basement now, and the Rudders' depression insurance apartment is not in use. Often these extra dwelling units are unofficial. They do not appear on the property description, and they are not included in assessing property tax. The City attempts to control and eliminate them on grounds that they often fail to meet local code and ordinance requirements for separate entries, independent kitchen and bath facilities, other physical building standards, or zoning regulations. Or, if they do meet requirements, the City wants to put them on the tax rolls. From the residents' point of view this seems an unreasonable intrusion, particularly in situations where they are providing temporary housing for kin and do not offer the apartments for rent on the open market.

South Austin

Thelma and Bill Johnson live in South Austin, a very different neighborhood from East Side. Originally a mixed working class and middle income neighborhood with large apartment buildings as well as many two- and three-flat buildings, South Austin has declined economically since the mid 1960s, and is now a low income neighborhood with high unemployment and significant physical deterioration. Almost all of the current residents are African-Americans who moved into the area since the late 1960s. The Johnsons bought their two-flat in 1967.

In 1983 Thelma, then 47, and her husband Bill, 53, her brother Allen, two of her granddaughters, Sasha, aged 10, and Chantelle, aged 9 (they are cousins), and her daughter-in-law, Mary (not either child's mother) lived on the second floor of the two-family house. Thelma's son, Charles, 27, and her 95-year old grandmother lived downstairs. Her mother lived nearby. All generations shared the house and contributed to its support as they could. Bill, Charles, and Mary were out of work. Allen, who is disabled, received social security. Thelma worked full-time as a nurse's aide in a nursing home and took on extra nursing jobs to help pay the bills. Bill found work in late 1983. In 1985 Gloria's grandmother died and shortly after Charles, now employed, moved to his own apartment so that in 1986 the downstairs was rented on the open market. Mary was able to move out to her own apartment in 1985. The house was emptying.

However, in 1984, Delia, seven months old, was added to the household. Delia is the daughter of Thelma's niece. Thelma recalls how the child came to the household.

> The mother left this baby with a girlfriend of hers. She went off, and was gone for three months. The girlfriend didn't know where the baby's mother was. You know how people talk to you and tell you how you can do that, you can do this. So what the girlfriend did, she went to Public Aid. She told Public Aid she needed money for the child, she needed medical costs for the child because she didn't have any money, and had no way to feed her or take care of her. So instead of Public Aid turning the mother's check over to her, they called up [the Department of] Children and Family Services and that is how they investigated. They took the baby. So when she told them about me, they call me; and I told them, yeah, that I was the baby's aunt. So they said do you want to take her? Or we will put her in a foster home. Well, I said, bring her to me.

In 1991 Thelma's nephew, Richard, then 14, joined the household. His family was deteriorating, his mother was using drugs, he was dropping out of school. So Thelma and Bill offered their home "to give him a better environment." Richard had lived with them temporarily before. In 1991 Allen moved to New Orleans to live with his uncle, and in 1992, Chantelle, then 18, moved out to live with her mother. Over the nine years we talked with Thelma, four members left the household to live elsewhere, two new members were added and one member died. This flexibility of household membership and openness of family boundaries seems very striking to persons whose experience is limited to conventional nuclear families, but it is common in the South Austin community. Taking in children, kin, near-kin and non-kin to improve their situation or to rescue them from the bureaucracy as Thelma Johnson did for Delia happens surprisingly often.

Willa Smith has also lived in South Austin since the mid-60s. She lives in a brick two-family house where the houses are set well back from the wide street. She lives on the second floor in a lavishly decorated five room apartment. She lived there alone when we first talked to her in 1983. Her daughter Sally and her grandson Todd lived downstairs. Sally paid her own electricity and gas, and Willa paid the heat for the downstairs and charged no rent. Sally was out of work because the company that employed her for 17 years had gone out of business in Chicago. Willa has been active in her local community all her life. She talks about how she raised four children who originally came to her through her neighborhood activity.

My children is adopted children, I have three, and they have a sister. She was older but I looked after her. I didn't adopt her, but I did take care of her until she could do it on her own. There was this man who had four children, and he was the worst father. He would go away and leave them children a whole week. There wasn't any food in the house. Then the neighbors took care of them, and the children would come up the street to see me. Then they would come over every Friday evening and they would stay with me. So one day the neighbors reported the father. Then they called me to bring them to Juvenile. I told the Judge, `You know, they are too little to be out in the street, and I have been taking care of them. I took them home and I fed them.' Juvenile Court told me to keep them until they could find a home for them. They wanted somebody that would take all of them. They couldn't find that. So the social work lady came back, and she asked me if I would keep them until they would adopt them out one by one. So I told her, 'If you are going to split them up, let them stay here. At least they can grow up loving one another.' It took me about six months or a year, but I adopted them and they never left.

Then I raised my sister's children in Ohio. My sister was sick. She lived in Ohio and she sent her three children here for me to keep. Now I have worked every day. I worked 33 years. I retired in 1977 from the company. And I kept those children. I sent them to school. When they got older and she got better, I sent them back.

When we last talked with Willa Smith in 1992 she was living alone upstairs. Her daughter Sally and grandson Todd, who had just graduated from high school and was preparing to go to college, still lived downstairs. But in the meantime others had come and gone in her household.

George, he was a friend to my grandson, well his mother, she just lost control of herself and she went off on her way and the father wasn't around. He made friends with Todd and was here off and on through the day and helping Todd. He didn't have no place to stay, and he started staying all night with Todd. So then he ask if he could stay here. I let him know the rules of my house and I let him know he has to abide by them. He stayed almost five years (1986-91). He graduated last year from here. If he needed something, a coat, a jacket or something, I bought it for him, and I fed him.

George had a sister who was also taken in by Willa.

First, she moved with a friend of hers, she had a little girl, then finally, she just didn't have no place to go and she came too, about a year after. So I told her, you stay until you get yourself together and you have your own place. I used to keep her little girl for her while she worked. She's keeping house now. She don't live too far; she comes by all the time.

After graduating from high school, George moved in with his stepfather and is working. While he and his sister are legally members of this other family, they have effectively become part of Willa's family as well. The children move back and forth freely between these two families.

Little Village

Originally home to immigrants from Eastern Europe, Little Village has been stable for some time, with a high percentage of home ownership in the two- and three-flat residences that crowd the small lots. Sylvia Rodriguez has owned a two-flat since 1974, shortly after arriving here from Mexico. She and her two children were deserted by her husband around 1980. She remarried in 1985 and continues to live in the same house. Her sister Margarita and her family moved into the downstairs apartment in 1986. In 1991 they were ready to move out, and were searching for a house of their own. They are the most recent of many relatives who have found shelter in the house, and for whom it has been a port of entry to new opportunity in the United States.

Her role as housing provider has changed Sylvia's status in the family from the role she could have expected as just one, and not the oldest, of many children. She says,

I'm the leader because I'm the one who has been living here longer. Almost all my family was not here from Mexico, and I have been the one to have them here at my house. Then once they find a job, and they are better off, they look for an apartment. My mother is jealous because she's been here for years, and she has a house. She asks why on Mother's Day everyone comes to my house; why everybody is always asking me what we are going to do?

Sharing

These stories illustrate two basic ways these households share housing. First, they make housing units available to others, usually but not only kin, often at nominal or no rent. Second, they change the composition of the household to accommodate others who would form independent households in other circumstances.

The changing and complex social relationships of reciprocity that bind household members to one another make shared housing possible and desirable. Contrast these stories with the unidimensional and functional notions of overcrowding often used to describe inner city housing. Taking a closer and more systematic look at household composition, change and house sharing for all the households in our study will show why we should be careful how we define housing need in poor neighborhoods.

Household Composition and House Sharing

We purposely designed our study to include four household types in addition to the nuclear family prototype of two adults and their children: single female-headed, all elderly, multi-generational and all adult. These categories of households can be reconciled with U.S. census classifications. However, census categories mask much diversity and many creative living arrangements. Assuming that any household containing persons who would usually be considered a separate household may be considered a situation of house sharing, we estimated the number of such sharing arrangements. The single adult mother and child living with the mother's parents is an obvious example.

We identified forms of household composition that suggest house sharing in 46 of the 89 households. Twenty households included extended kin, and 26 households included at least one adult child. So almost two out of five dwellings (39 percent) harbored one or more potentially independent households. If the people composing these households lived in separate dwellings, an additional 54 households would have been formed from among the 89 households we studied in 1985.

The distribution of such households tended to vary with community area (see Table 2). About half of the African-American respondents in the South Austin neighborhood reported sheltering extended kin or adult children, while only slightly more than a quarter of the households of the white ethnic respondents in the East Side neighborhood shared their dwellings, virtually all with adult children. About 40 percent of the Hispanic households in Little Village included adult children or extended kin in equal proportions.

TABLE 2
Estimates for Number of Potential Households Sharing the Same Dwelling with Other Households

Community	Total Hshlds	Extnd Kin	Adult Child	Net Share	Potential New Hshlds
South Austin	35	11	13	17	31
East Side	28	3	7	8	10
Little Village	26	6	6	10	13
Total	89	20	26	35	54

Note: Extended kin indicates households including relatives or friends not related to the interview respondent by marriage or birth. Adult child indicates households including children of the respondent 21 years of age or older. In many cases, a household would include both extended kin and an adult child. Such households were only counted once and tallied in the net share column. The final column lists the total number of potential households hypothetically generated from the households in the net total. In other words, 35 of the 89 dwellings were shared, and these included an estimated potential of 54 new households.

While house sharing represents an important source of help for the tenant, we found that the helping relation flowed both ways. Household members, including older children, extended kin, or friends who share accommodations, frequently contribute to the maintenance and security of the household. Most of the households rely on these other members to pay bills and care for dependents.

The type and frequency of helping within these households varies by household type. For example, nuclear households most resemble the traditional notion of household management (see Table 3). On average only one of the two adults is responsible for paying the rent and utilities in nuclear households, and only one of the household members is responsible for housework and caring for someone in the house who might be ill or need other care. Typically the man provides the money, and the woman provides the maintenance and care. For all other household types more members contribute more frequently to household maintenance. In households composed exclusively of adults, virtually everyone contributes financial support and direct service. Multi-generation and single-parent households rely on children for a lot of the housework and a high percentage of the adults provide financial contributions. The importance of pooling resources and effort to the well-being of these households is obvious.

TABLE 3
Contributions to Household Support within the Households, 1985

| | *Adults and Elderly Contribute to* | | *Percent All Contribute to* | |
	Rent	*Utilities*	*Housework*	*Care*
Household Type				
Elderly	58	92	100	43
Multi-generation	59	62	68	62
Single Parent	81	72	74	49
Nuclear	50	55	55	49
All Adult	68	88	73	80

Note: Children do not typically contribute money to household support.

Household Change

The particular arrangements for house sharing that existed among these households in 1985 is a snapshot of an ongoing, dynamic process of household change including change in type, size and membership. Some of the arrangements are very recent; some are long lived. Half of the 89 households had changed members during the 24 months between summer 1983 and summer 1985. While some lost, others gained and still other households both lost and gained.

Many households changed in size—babies were born, a few persons died, a few left home to marry, and relatives, most often nieces, nephews, uncles, and grandchildren, moved in and out. Often these changes did not appear to greatly affect the dynamic of household management. For many families, moves between households were pragmatic solutions to problems of illness or unemployment. For instance, a nuclear household of adults and children took in a new baby, a 30-year old father, and a 50-year old mother-in-law. The boundaries of "family" stretched for this household, and they pooled resources to accommodate these new relationships.

The single-parent households changed with the birth of additional children, the return of children who had been living with other family members, and as others' children were taken in. A quarter of the single-parent households grew smaller as children moved out; simultaneously a quarter of them had a net increase in number of members. For instance, two births to high school age daughters living with mothers changed what had been single-parent households in 1983 into multi-generation households in 1985 with grandmother, daughter, and grandchildren living together.

Nuclear households were most likely to change as children moved in or out of the parental nest. For instance, one nuclear household changed in several ways. A young adult daughter married and moved out; her parents divorced and chose to live separately. Such occurrences were rare. Elderly households in our study were most stable: two of nine lost members. From time to time elderly households take in new members—elderly friends or relatives—but none of this occurred from 1983 to 1985 in the study's elderly household population.

Multi-generation households most often acquired new children or lost adult members. For example, one multi-generation household welcomed a new baby but also felt it necessary to place an elderly member of the household in a mental hospital. The household remained multi-generational, but their lives have changed greatly. This family now relies on a mixture of employment income, AFDC, and help from relatives.

The institution of the extended family seems to be the key to viewing household change for these households. On the aggregate, the surface picture is one of stability; the 'household type' composition of our study population was stable. However, this aggregate stability masks change in the membership and living arrangements of more than half of the households, with most changes involving extended family.

House Sharing and Informal and Formal Help

The house sharing that these households do, and the helping among household members with the management, maintenance, and support of the house, take place within a larger context of relatively frequent informal help among relatives, friends, and neighbors.

Many close relationships are mainly social, but many also involve both giving and getting material and financial assistance and advice and help with daily problems such as household maintenance, child care, and transportation. As shown in Table 4 the households identified 439 informal helping relationships in 1985.

TABLE 4
Informal Helping Relations by Type of Relation, 1985

	Kind of Interaction				
	Get Help	Give Help	Equal Helping	Not Much Helping	Total Relations
Relatives	36	36	101	66	239
Friends	34	7	67	37	145
Neighbors	5	4	33	13	55
Total	75	47	201	116	439

Informal help is not evenly distributed among household types. Relationships defined mainly by getting help were concentrated among elderly and multigenerational households. Adult households were most likely to report relationships in which the respondent gave more than they got. Reciprocal helping ties predominated among single-parent and nuclear households. However, the size of the helping networks for respondents in single-parent households was significantly smaller (2.9 helping relationships) than those of respondents in nuclear households (4.4).

Money is the most common type of help exchanged informally. Help with shopping trips and child care comes next in frequency followed by exchange of food, advice, and help with car and house repairs. Many of these exchanges clearly involve minor daily problems, but others may be more crucial to the functioning of the household.

In contrast with informal helping, these households go to public agencies, nonprofit organizations and membership organizations far less often for help with their problems. During 1985 these 89 households reported contacting 77 agencies and nonprofit organizations for help and actually requesting help from 63 of them. Two-thirds of the instances of formal agency help were from public agencies; one-third was from nonprofit organizations. In addition to help from agencies, these households get help from membership organizations to which they belong. These include social clubs, churches, civic organizations, and block clubs, among others. Respondents reported fifteen instances of getting help from such organizations in 1985. As might be expected, traditional nuclear households and households with employed members were more likely to belong to and draw support from membership organizations.

Like helping between relatives, friends, and neighbors, membership organizations involve reciprocal relations. The 89 households reported belonging to 80 membership organizations in 1985. While they received help from them fifteen times, they also gave help to these organizations through volunteering their services 20 times.

Food was the most common type of help these households got from all formal sources (23 instances). Combined with meals this accounts for one-third of all the formal help received. About one-sixth of the help is health services and another one-sixth is advice and counseling for a variety of problems. Money help is relatively infrequent (four instances of help). No help with housing was reported. It appears that emergency help with a material crisis—food, meals, and money—is the primary reason these households go to agencies. Health services which probably cannot be gotten from informal sources are second, but only half as frequent as emergency services and no more frequent than advice and counseling.

Why Households Help

These households engage in a great variety of helping within and outside of the house, among family and others, and in sharing their houses. At the same time they make relatively modest use of services provided by public and non-profit agencies. Yet these people clearly need help coping with life's problems. By any standard measure they have major unmet needs. On average they are low to very low income. What then explains their behavior? While we cannot attempt to answer this very complex question here, we can offer some suggestions.

First, the conventional understanding of the relationship between need and dependence suggests that increases in household vulnerability or need would correlate positively with the incidence of informal help among household members. If household needs and helping are closely tied, then we expect to find the proportion of household members engaging in helping behavior to vary with changes between 1983 and 1985 in the vulnerability of the household and changes in the economy and availability of public services. We tested this conventional view using the regression models in Table 5. The models measure household vulnerability in terms of household earnings (percent adults receive earnings income), dependents (percent members <18 and >65 years of age), and health conditions (percent members with acute or chronic illness in previous year) on the three measures of informal helping among household members. The models also control for the effects of household vulnerability in 1985, household type, and neighborhood location.

Active helping within households includes caring for other members, contributing money to help pay utilities/rent, and helping perform household chores. We adjusted these measures to control for household size: the percent of all adults (members > 18 years of age) who cared for others in the household, the percent of dependents performing household chores, and the percent of all adults helping to pay rent/utilities. These represent the dependent variables in the regression models.

Only one measure of change exhibited an effect on household help. Households reporting an increasing proportion of unhealthy members between 1983 and 1985 were likely to report a smaller portion of dependents performing chores, since ill members are less likely to do chores. The analysis shows that in these households, changes in the fortune of the household does not predict the scope of helping within households. The only significant statistical correlations are weak and involve common sense associations, for example an increase in illness in the household is linked with less participation in household help.

TABLE 5

Effects of Household Resources and Vulnerability on Informal Helping Among Household Members (Estimated Using Regression Models)

Independent Variables	% Adults Care for Others	% Dependents Do Hshld Chores	% Adults Pay Rent/Utilities
Intercept	.87*	.26*	.30*
1985 Values			
Earnings	-.07	-.21	.44*
Aid	.04	-.14	.70*
Dependents	.10	.65*	-.25
Ill Health	-.11	.06	.01
83–85 Change			
Earn rate	-.03	.04	-.06
Aid rate	-.04	.04	-.11
Dependent rate	-.01	-.13	.04
Health rate	-.08	-.20+	-.03
Control Values			
Elderly	-.75*	.25	.23
Community	-.25*	-.12	-.00
R2	.44	.37	.54
F	`6.2*	4.5*	9.3*

Note: + <.05; * <.01

Although changes in household vulnerability between 1983 and 1985 had little relation to the extent of different types of active help within households, some measures of household vulnerability for 1985 did. Dependents were not only indicators of need, but contributors to household well-being. The more dependents made up a household, the greater the proportion of dependents who helped out. Similarly, more adults were likely to help defray rent and utility expenses in households with a high percent age of employed adults, regardless of dependency or health levels.

Listening to the persons we interviewed suggests a different direction for seeking an explanation of sharing in these households. Willa Smith credits her mother for teaching her to care for others, especially children. She tells this story of her childhood in Georgia:

> My mother raised two children that wasn't hers because of her kind heart and the feelings she had for other people. It happened like this. This lady passed. She liked my mother and she told the mailman in the rural route at that time to tell my mother to come see her because she was sick and she had something to tell her. I was a little girl. Well my mother didn't go that day. She went two days later. My mother got the man right below us, he had an old-time piece of car, you know, one of those jalopies. She got him to take her up to this lady's house which was twelve miles from where we lived. And she told my mother, 'What's taking you so long, Janie?' So she said, 'I just had things to do'. My father was dead at that time; my mother had six children to raise, and it was hard to do. She said, 'Janie, what I want from you is I want you to take my two children and raise them.' She said, 'Oh no! The woman said, 'Take them.' Well, my mother told her she would take her children and do best she could for them. If she had anything for her own, she is going to have enough for them too or they would all starve together. My mother raised them right along with us, and if she didn't have money to buy all of us something, whichever one needed, she would get it. My adopted sister, she bought her a pair of socks and let me do without it if I had any. So at the table, she overheard us talking about it. I mean about buying for the lady's two children, their getting stuff, and she didn't like what we were saying. So she said, 'I am going to tell you all something.' She said, 'Do you think it is too much to share your mother with somebody that don't have a mother or father?' She said, 'It is a shame. I thought you all thought better than that. I'm ashamed of you.' She shamed us out of it. We never did that again.

Both in these personal interviews and in later focus groups we conducted with our respondents to explore motivation for helping, family tradition, lessons learned from parents, the prevailing norms of the local community in which they grew up, and religious teachings were credited as the source of their helping behavior. Roberta's story of parental instruction by example was repeated in many forms. Religious sayings from both

Protestant and Catholic upbringing were often used to explain their helping. Folk sayings from ethnic, racial, and national sources were similarly used. Most of the respondents internalized these influences in two ways. First, a person's quality was defined by their willingness to share with others. A person who did not share with others in the community was described as unhappy and lacking in humanity. Second, the respondents individually experienced good feelings about themselves as a consequence of living up to these norms of sharing. There were variations in degree of commitment to sharing and in specific influences among the African-American, Hispanic, and white respondents, but they all cited the same sources.

Conclusion

These observations do not prove that sharing is widespread or that it is a preferred behavior. Many of those sharing housing might be pleased to have independent housing. Further, it would be inappropriate to conclude that willing sharing, including house sharing, occurs only among low income households. However, house sharing does exist among these low income households with surprising frequency given our national pattern of decreasing household size and increasing household formation. Our respondents appear to regard house sharing positively and to accept it as part of their lives, rather than think of it as temporary and as an indication of failure.

Housing is shared for a variety of reasons. At least four stand out, although individual instances may combine several of these reasons.

Emergency Need. Households take in others for temporary periods to help them cope with a variety of calamities.

Dependency. Some persons are unable to provide for themselves, often due to age or infirmity, and are housed by others.

Subsidy. Sometimes people help others (especially kin) with housing to improve their standard of living and/or well-being.

Growth and Change. People share housing as an element in a strategy to change their life circumstances.

House sharing is widespread among the households we interviewed. However, it is only one part of a larger pattern of informal helping which appears to be an integral part of their lives and important to their standard and quality of life. That house sharing is embedded in a context of informal helping is important to understanding why it does and does not exist among different groups. This embeddedness will be an important consideration in any public policy efforts to support shared housing.

CHAPTER 3

Informal Additions to the U.S. Housing Stock: Changing Structures and Changing Uses

Anna Hardman

The vast majority of dwellings added to the housing stock in the United States today are part of what housing researchers call the formal sector: construction firms build dwellings that comply with local building, zoning, and subdivision codes. But a substantial portion of additions to the housing stock come from informal sources. Informal additions occur when buildings and units move into the housing supply from non-residential uses, or from rehabilitated structures previously condemned as not habitable, or when an existing unit is subdivided into two or more smaller units. This chapter estimates from published Census Bureau data the magnitude of informal additions to the housing stock and identifies ways to measure the contribution of informal sector housing in the United States by tracking its additions and losses affecting total housing stock. The limited data now available provide ample evidence that informal housing represents a significant, if overlooked, portion of housing supply in many U.S. housing markets.

Informal housing is the term used to describe the illegal ways that households find or create shelter in third world cities: squatting and housing construction on vacant land owned by others; illegal subdivision and substandard housing development on land zoned for other uses; and illegal addition of rooms or units to existing structures. The informal sector attracted attention because it became clear that these activities, which had been neglected as insignificant, made up a large part of the housing supply in third world cities.[1]

This concept of informal additions draws attention to a corresponding set of activities in the United States housing sector, until now largely ignored by both researchers and policy-makers. The narrowest definition of this sector includes only units that are added without a building permit.[2] A broader definition includes many more kinds of illegal use: rental apartments whose landlord does not declare income from the units to the IRS, public housing units that illegally house extended family members or roomers, owner-financed sales of housing and informal rooming house arrangements in single family dwellings.

The providers, who usually operate on a small scale, evade regulations, permitting procedures, zoning codes, building codes, permit requirements, and local licensing rules. For example, a home owner creates an accessory apartment without a building permit in a neighborhood zoned only for one-family dwellings. Other examples that would fall into the informal sector include a dwelling with more unrelated residents than the local code allows; an unlicensed home business such as a bed-and-breakfast or family day care; and even a mobile home owner who fails to meet local code requirements. Marginal cases would include a landlord who charges a rent higher than that allowed under local rent control laws, or a condominium owner who violates residents' association rules by renting out the unit.

Changes in tenure and use, as well as structural changes, can make a unit informal, but while the definition of informal sector used in this chapter includes changes between non-residential and residential uses, it excludes changes in tenure.[3] Using currently available Census Bureau data we can identify changes in the housing stock which are more likely to be informal—the category of "other additions".

Informal Housing in the United States

Baer (1986) describes changing use and tenure within the existing housing stock as "churning", a label that implies useless or wasteful change. But informal changes in the use of existing housing often respond to current shifts in local housing demand more quickly than formal new construction. These informal adaptations frequently violate local land use regulations which make otherwise useful conversions illegal. Even new construction may be part of the informal sector when it is built without permits in a locality which requires them. Some of the construction labor used in small projects may be hired informally, or "off the books" particularly when the owner does not hire a general contractor.[4] Analysts have tended to neglect the study of informal sector housing, viewing it as a marginal and otherwise unacceptable form of housing that should eventually give way to more formal, conventional forms of housing. Census takers, influenced by this belief, tend to count new construction of conventional housing while relegating the reuse of existing housing to the category of "other".[5]

We usually assume that data collection methods are more accurate in developed than in developing countries.[6] This may not be the case.

Between 1970 and 1980 the U.S. Census showed that the number of U.S. households had grown by 17 million. During the same period 20.3 million housing units were added through new construction and 7.2 million units were lost, yielding a net increase of only 13.1 million new housing units. Thus, four million households, almost 25 percent of the total increase, found housing through means other than new construction. Change in vacancy rates was inadequate to explain the discrepancy. Where did these households go? The Census Bureau explained that the surplus households were accommodated through the creation of 4.9 million "unspecified units", additions to the stock which were not measured by the Construction Reports series of the Bureau's Housing Statistics Division (Gordon 1987: 3).

The only source of information about change in the national housing stock other than new construction is a little-known Census Bureau survey called the Components of Inventory Change (CINCH), conducted as part of the American Housing Survey.[7] Unfortunately, the census publishes only tabulations and does not make micro-data for the CINCH available to researchers. This chapter uses the most recent CINCH data available in 1994, which were the 1973–83 Components of Inventory Change published in 1991.[8]

TABLE 6

United States Housing Inventory Changes
1973–1983 (in thousands of units)

Type of Housing Stock	Additions to Inventory	Losses From Inventory	Net Change
Housing Stock Unchanged	70,739	—	—
Conventional Construction			
Housing Stock	16,171	2,444	13,727
Mobile homes	3,754	2,233	1,521
Other Changes			
Conversion	1,108	499	609
Merger	602	1,149	<507>
Nonresidential	1,088	596	492
Group quarters	721	189	532
Retrievable losses	238	633	<395>
Total Other	3,757	3,046	691
Total Net Change	23,682	7,743	15,939

Note: Each type of change in the "Other Changes" category measures a component of change. For instance, the 1.108 million conversions in the Additions column measure the number of new dwellings due to the subdivision of existing units between 1973 and 1983. The 499 thousand units in the Losses column counts the number of dwelling units that remain in 1983 after merging dwellings subdivided before 1973 into fewer units. A conversion into two units results in a gross loss of one unit and a net gain of one unit, while a merger of two units into one results in a net loss of one unit. One conversion and one merger does not change the net number of units.

Table 6 outlines additions and losses to the U.S. housing stock between 1973 and 1983. The table distinguishes between two very different sources of change to the housing stock: gains and losses in conventional dwellings such as houses, apartments and mobile homes, and changes to existing units due to such activities as conversion or merger. A more detailed description for each type follows.

Stock Unchanged and New Construction

Until recently, research on changes in the stock of housing concentrated on new construction because housing is a very durable commodity: dwellings deteriorate slowly even if they are not maintained. In any one year or even decade, the overwhelming majority of dwelling units in the country are not modified structurally. We tend to believe that building permit data gives us a fairly accurate idea of how much the housing stock is changing and how much new residential construction is underway. Building permits tell us how many new dwellings are added to the housing stock from year to year, and gives us some information on renovations of and modifications to existing housing. But it is new construction data that is included by the Census Bureau in its construction statistics.

PERMANENT LOSSES

Permanent losses are units that disappear from the stock. They are housing units that are demolished, or so totally destroyed by fire, or by natural disasters, that there is no hope of making them habitable again.

MOBILE HOMES

Nearly all the dwellings moved in or out are mobile homes—inexpensive, usually owner-occupied units often neglected in studies of additions to housing stock. Sellers of new mobile homes are commonly required to deliver them to lots with water and sanitation, but as planning officials in one rural Virginia county report, used mobile homes can become informal housing when moved to new sites (often invisible from the road) which do not meet code requirements.[9]

CONVERSIONS AND MERGERS

Conversions and mergers change the number of units in the housing stock, but aside from basement and attic renovation, the floor area used for housing typically changes little, if at all. Conversions are defined as modifications to structure which create more units than before. The Census Bureau definition includes the conversion of the basement or attic of a single-family house into an additional dwelling unit (a popular way of creating an accessory apartment). Mergers are changes to the existing residential stock that convert a number of smaller units into fewer larger ones. For example, a single-family dwelling may be created from a two-family dwelling or single-family dwelling with an accessory unit.

NON-RESIDENTIAL

Additions to the housing stock from non-residential use, or losses from the stock to non-residential use, are a heterogeneous category. The estimated number of additions from non-residential uses appears large, but the numbers reported by the Census Bureau may also be misleading because it defines a unit created in the basement of a one-family house as a conversion; an extra unit created in the basement of a two-family or a three-family house is classified as an addition from non-residential use. Other obvious kinds of additions from non-residential use are conversions of older structures such as shops, schools, old factories, and even churches into housing. A formerly residential structure used as work space (studios or offices) by people who do not live there is classified as a loss to non-residential use.

In countries where change of use is unregulated, neighborhoods make a transition over time from residential to non-residential uses. In this country such changes of use are quite strictly regulated. Therefore we might classify changes of use without zoning approval as informal because they contravene local regulations, such as a business which starts with a home office and gradually expands to involve the whole dwelling.

GROUP QUARTERS

Group quarters are the dwellings where large numbers or groups of people live but do not have individual dwelling units though they may have private space of some sort. This category includes single-room-occupancy hotels (SROs), hospitals, dormitories, fraternities, and sororities. There is movement between group quarters and household residential uses, but again some of these changes may reflect the arbitrary nature of the categories. The classification of a group of ten friends living in a large single family house as group quarters or a household depends on whether the person being interviewed reports honestly the number of residents, how many are related, and whether they eat meals together. Many group quarters are large institutional structures and movement into or out of the housing stock occurs when major investments are made to transform them into individual dwelling units.

RETRIEVABLE LOSSES

Retrievable losses, a significant source of additions as well as losses, are units with repairable damage from fire, natural disasters, or deterioration and abandonment. Some of these units exit the housing stock temporarily, returning to the housing stock after repair. The repaired units are not tabulated as additions in the data on building permits for new construction, even if the owners get building permits. The retrievable losses category, then, is a neglected potential source of information on informal additions.

Comparing the Sources of Change in the U.S. Housing Stock

Between 1973 and 1983 more than three out of four housing units (70.7 million dwellings) remained unchanged in the United States (see Table 6). Conventional new construction (16.2 million) accounted for twice as many additions as other sources (7.5 million). However, losses from other sources (5.3 million) were more than twice the size of permanent losses from the conventional housing stock (2.4 million). The loss of mobile homes contributed most to this difference. Gains and losses among the unconventional sources other than mobile homes tended to even out in aggregate, but with large differences among components. As one would expect, conversions added and mergers removed units from the housing stock (usually by one unit), while only about a quarter of the potentially retrievable losses were realized. The large net additions due to the conversion of nonresidential units to dwellings and the conversion of dwellings to group quarters were especially noteworthy.[10]

The national numbers conceal wide variation in change among geographic areas. Central city areas, usually with an older housing stock and little vacant land, tended to capture a much smaller share of conventional new housing units than their fast growing suburban areas. Rural and small town areas showed a robust growth in conventional housing, as well as in the provision of new mobile homes. Unconventional additions through conversion or other forms of residential re-use accounted for almost a third (32 percent) of the total additions in central cities, but much smaller portions of total suburban (21 percent) and rural (13.2 percent) additions respectively. Suburban areas outside central cities offered plenty of vacant land to absorb new housing developments and permanent losses there were relatively few compared to the volume of new construction. But still, even in these growth centers a significant amount of housing was added through unconventional means.

Additions from conversion were greatest in the central cities of the Northeast. Between 1973 and 1983, the modest new construction of 257 thousand units in the central cities of the Northeast was almost offset by permanent losses of 252 thousand (see Table 7). This net contribution of five thousand units was dwarfed by changes to the existing stock that added some 75,000 units. The subdivision of dwellings, creation of group quarters, and conversion of non-residential structures to residential use more than made up for failure to make good on retrievable losses. But who lived in this housing and who was doing the conversion?

TABLE 7

Housing Inventory Changes Northeast Region - Central Cities
1973–1983 (in 1000's of units)

Type of Housing Stock	Additions to Inventory	Losses From Inventory	Net Change
Housing stock unchanged	—	—	7,198
Conventional additions/losses			
Housing	257	252	5
Mobile Homes	2	2	0
Other Changes to Inventory			
Conversion	150	71	79
Merger	104	228	<124>
Non-residential	261	36	225
Group quarters	48	24	24
Retrievable losses	34	163	<129>
Total other	599	524	80

Characteristics of Owners, Units, and Occupants in Informal Units

Small scale is a basic characteristic of the informal sector. Those most likely to be subdividing or merging dwellings and converting non-residential spaces to residential use are owner-occupiers, extended family, and small landlords. Tenants are much less likely to have an informal contract or to live in an informal unit if their landlord owns more than a few units. The question of identifying informal additions or non-new additions to the housing stock is inseparable from the characteristics of the owners of these informal additions. At the same time, we know relatively little about who owns the housing stock in this country and even less about the owners of "other additions".

To understand what the units created by other additions are like and who lives in them, we can examine unit and occupant characteristics of the "other additions" to the housing stock created between 1973 and 1983. The published Census Bureau data give only general information, but we can compare the occupants and structures in new housing with those in conversions, mergers, and an "other" category which includes additions from non-residential uses, additions from group quarters, and mobile homes moved into the survey area. Smaller scale, locally based studies provide further information about the proportion of these units that are likely to be "informal", who makes the conversions, and who lives in the informal units.

TABLE 8
United States Housing Units Created
1973–1983
General Characteristics in 1983

	New	Conversion	Merger	Other
Owner-occupied	69.2	30.2	74.3	53.5
Renter	30.8	69.8	25.7	46.5
Median number of units in structure	1	3	1	1
Median year structure built	>1973	<1939	<1939	1970
Median number of rooms				
Owners	5.2	3.7	6.5	3.9
Renters	4.0	3.4	5.2	3.6
Persons per unit				
Owners	3.1	2.1	3.0	2.3
Renters	1.9	1.7	3.0	1.8
Percent Black				
Owners	4.2	9.3	19.3	6.1
Renters	10.0	14.8	28.6	14.4

Table 8 summarizes unit characteristics of the national housing stock between 1973 and 1983. Of rented stock, subdivided dwellings proved more numerous (69.8 percent) than mergers (46.5 percent) or other kinds of housing additions (46.5 percent). In all cases, except mergers, owners had more people per unit on average than renters. In other words, households that purchased new dwellings between 1973 and 1983 were larger on average than those who rented. Mergers are typically accessory apartments or secondary units previously created to generate rent for small landlords which are subsequently restored to single family use. Not surprisingly, the merged units tended to possess more (6.5) rooms than any other type of housing addition, including new construction. This signifies an important resource for many large renter households. Whereas the average person per unit for new rental units was less than two (1.9 per unit), the average was three for households renting the large merged units. Conversions and mergers occurred mainly for housing built before 1939 and concentrated in older central cities. Blacks were far more likely to rent converted (14.4 percent) or merged (28.6 percent) dwellings than newly constructed apartments (10 percent). Many home owners in black inner city neighborhoods were meeting household and economic needs by subdividing or consolidating rooms in relatively small older buildings.

Informal Conversion in Boston

Conversion activity in Boston occurs mainly through informal means by owners of small dwellings. Distinguishing "professional owners" who usually possess large residential holdings from "amateur investors" who manage only a few rental units, Sagalyn (1982) found that the professionals controlled a much smaller portion of the Boston rental stock than commonly believed. Professional investors owned only 57 percent of rental housing. Among the amateur investors, resident owners (Boston residents who own one or more apartments in the city) controlled 41 percent of the Boston rental stock, while resident investors (who own rental units in the same building in which they reside) controlled about two percent. Amateur investors and not professionals do most of the conversion. Much of the conversion activity goes unreported.

In 1985 the Boston Redevelopment Authority studied conversion activity in three neighborhoods (South End, Jamaica Plain and Allston Brighton) where reports of illegal conversions were high (Gordon 1987). Analysts conducted in depth interviews with a random sample of 600 homeowners of whom 48 (eight percent) were converters who still lived on the premises.[11]

Conversion activity was concentrated. More than one in four homeowners in the South End reported adding one or more units, compared with only four percent in Jamaica Plain and two percent in Allston-Brighton. In the South End half of the non-converters had witnessed conversion activity nearby during the past five years, compared to about a fifth of the non-converters in the other neighborhoods. Reports of conversion activity in Jamaica Plain and Allston-Brighton are probably due less to the vigilance of the neighbors than the presence of converters who did not participate in the survey. Since much of the conversion is illegal, converters who know the law would likely avoid participating in a survey that might lead to detection. In fact, nearly half of the conversion carried out by homeowners was undertaken illegally. Yet most of the participating converters (91 percent) reported that they did not believe their conversions required regulatory approval. While a few added independent dwellings to their properties without obtaining a building permit, most obtained a building permit but failed to obtain a variance or conditional use permit from the Board of Zoning Appeal.

In most municipalities, adding additional units to a dwelling requires an approved variance from the existing zoning rules. Local government inspectors usually identify cases of illegal additions by following up on neighbors' complaints. Zoning boards often use the presence or absence of neighbor disapproval as a test of whether to approve or deny an application for a variance. While the creation and rental of illegal units benefits both the owner and tenant, the neighbors are potentially adversely affected. Furthermore, this type of enforcement saves the costs of directly maintaining compliance with the law. The Boston Board of Zoning Appeal typically approved requests for ex-post legalization of converted apartments where notified neighbors did not object, and rejected those where neighbors appeared at the hearings to protest.[12]

Variances are difficult to obtain and risky. Owners who know the rules and avoid obtaining a variance will convert covertly and illegally. These owners show up before the Board of Appeals, if at all, when selling their house, hoping to realize greater sales value due to the presence of a legal rental unit. Legalization of an existing illegal unit is one of the most common cases heard before the Boston Board of Zoning Appeal. In 1984, more units were legalized in previously converted buildings (208) than were approved for conversion (170).[13]

Most of the converters who failed to obtain a variance out of ignorance of legal procedure could have done so only with the tacit approval of a building inspector. Four out of five of the illegal converters took out building permits for conversion plans that inspectors examined and approved. Either the permit applicant withheld information about the planned change of occupancy or the inspectors looked the other way. Owners can omit their intent to change the occupancy and use of their property when filling out the building permit. In such cases building inspectors will simply inspect for safety rather than violation of use. Owners can also obtain building permits for electrical and plumbing work at different times over an extended period. Such incremental requests can be carefully managed to avoid the suspicion of building inspectors who might otherwise suspect conversion.

Statistics on the size of projects submitted to the Boston Board of Zoning Appeal suggest that smaller conversion projects are accomplished illegally, or slip through the system unnoticed by building inspectors, while larger conversion projects are over-represented among legal conversions. Among projects submitted for prior approval to the Board, almost two units on average were to be added to each of the converted single-family structures, and an average of 1.6 units were added to each two-family building. Large multi-family apartment buildings were reconfigured to make room for an additional 6.6 units, on average. It is easier for small landlords to evade regulations than large builders.

The converters who applied for a variance usually received it. Only about a quarter complained that they had difficulty obtaining a variance. However, the average processing time was 3.4 months, with one owner waiting a year before receiving approval. Most legal converters successfully obtained approval for their additions, while illegal converters successfully avoided the rules. Only 11 percent of the homeowners who had planned to add a unit and had not done so offered regulatory restrictions as the reason they dropped the idea. Zoning regulations do not appear to constrain the supply of conversions in Boston.

Conclusions

Conversions and mergers put the durability and malleability of the housing stock to use. As small owners in particular divide and consolidate their holdings in response to household and economic changes, they expand or contract the availability of shared accommodations through informal and frequently illegal means. These informal changes help stabilize housing prices by providing ways to adapt the existing housing stock to meet new demands. Conversions and mergers tend to even out in aggregate, but they offer important housing improvements when analyzed across different geographic areas. Conversions help meet demand for small rentals in older growing neighborhoods, while mergers offer large affordable rental dwellings for big households in older neighborhoods.

Informal additions are a significant source of housing supply about which we know too little. The scant evidence suggests that conversions, mergers, and group quarters play an important role in meeting the housing needs of changing households. But we still know too little about how these dwellings are produced and how the occupants use them. Do people choose these dwellings out of necessity or choice? Do the owners who convert do so strictly for economic reasons or to provide shelter for extended family or friends? Who are the small scale converters who become resident landlords? How common are temporary conversions as an income source for the divorced, elderly, or unemployed? What factors influence the impact of additions on neighbors and on the neighborhood? How might current regulatory policies that often discourage residential conversion be modified to encourage it? There are many questions worthy of careful research attention.

At a minimum we would do well to reconsider popular beliefs about the uniformity and desirability of the U.S. housing stock. Millions of households live in dwellings that do not fit the conventional classification of house or apartment. Formal and informal adaptive reuse of existing housing represents a legitimate and desirable alternative to more conventional choices. Regulation which discourages such re-use increases the cost of housing by making the existing stock less malleable.

Notes

1. In an influential paper, Peattie points out that the concept has played an important role in development theory and policy because it gave "standing" to "a bundle of miscellaneous activities" which had previously been ignored. She argues that it did so even though the "informal sector" is a "fuzzy" concept, and one which has been used in many ways, in part because it has served as a "banner" which appeals to different groups with conflicting purposes, but that it does not serve as an adequate basis for policy-making:

> It is important, in developing housing policies for the Third World countries, to note that most dwelling units are produced by very small enterprises, often involving self-contracting and owner participation in the building process. But to give a name to these activities, to lump them together as the informal sector, is not to have a clear comprehension of them . . . The "informal sector", however defined, is not necessarily a category within which to locate the poor. (Gordon 1987: 857–858)

2. One of the most appealing euphemisms for illegal housing that I have encountered was used in an English study which talked about dwellings "beyond the purview of local planning authorities".

3. The published census data do not allow us to disaggregate structural changes and changes in use.

4. While in many third world cities most of the informal housing added is new construction, a recent OECD report points out that "informality through subcontracting is spreading in the advanced industrial countries as well as in the third world" (Lubell 1991: 14).

5. In estimating the volume of all new dwellings completed and under construction, the Census Bureau assumes that some are informal sector, though it does not identify them as such. It adds 3.3% to the

estimated number of new single family dwellings completed in areas where permits are required, "to account for those units built within permit-issuing areas but without permit authorization" (Current Construction Reports: Housing Completions, January 1993 Bureau of the Census, Washington, D.C., March 1993, p. 8). In published Census documentation no basis is given for the adoption of 3.3% as the adjustment figure. An unpublished study carried out by the Bureau of the Census in 1964 justifies both the 3.3% figure and the assumption that only single family housing is built without permits by citing a "study spanning a four-year period" which "indicated that permits were obtained for buildings with two housing units or more". The memorandum describing the study is "Results of Permit Coverage Survey 1962–3" by Virginia Bell, October 9, 1964. The survey method is described in detail in U.S. Department of Commerce, Bureau of the Census, Survey of Permit Coverage Enumerator's Manual. Form 16–150, dated 4/1/60.

6. But, see Morgenstern 1963.

7. In 1940 the Bureau of Labor Statistics undertook a survey of additions to the housing stock in an attempt to reconcile building permit data on housing units added to the stock with the much larger observed changes in the number of households. Until 1970 the Components of Inventory Change survey was administered as part of the decennial Census of Housing. Since 1970, it has been part of the biennial American Housing Survey.

8. Any type of illegal or informal activity is inherently difficult to survey or to research. The data may undercount illegal units or miss them entirely. There are three possible sources of error in the CINCH data.

The first problem involves sampling. The AHS tracks units from one survey to the next, potentially allowing us to follow the history of individual dwelling units. However, the method used to identify additions uses building permits. It is questionable whether the AHS administration has been able to identify and include in the AHS sample an appropriate number of new units or units added from the non-residential stock which may not have permits. Thus it will certainly undercount some categories of informal housing.

The second problem is misreporting. People involved in activities that are illegal, or at least in a gray area "beyond the purview of the local authorities", have good reasons to try to conceal the truth. For example, a homeowner who has a tenant and who lives in a neighborhood zoned for single family housing may not admit to the AHS interviewer that she has added an accessory unit. People who are in irregular situations are more likely to refuse to respond and more likely not to tell the truth than people who are obeying the law. This is a special concern when informal sector activities are precisely the kind of behavior in which we are most interested.

If anything, other additions are likely to be under-estimated relative to losses: this kind of data collection makes it virtually certain that all losses will be identified and less likely that all additions will be included. For example, mergers—such as the conversion of two smaller units into one larger unit and thus representing two losses and one addition—are less likely to be misreported than conversions because mergers do not contravene zoning codes in most jurisdictions, whereas conversions often do because they add units.

The third problem is that the Census Bureau's definition of unchanged units does not count temporary uses between decennial surveys. For example, a dwelling that was single-family in 1973, became a duplex, and then returned to single-family use before 1983 would be counted as unchanged in the 1983 survey. This hides the informal additions to the housing stock and flows of housing units into and out of the housing stock, and the ways accessory units or within their dwellings. However, now that the surveys are being done every two years, the problem is much less serious, and the Census Bureau is now careful to warn that summing 10 years of biennial changes does not give the same 10 year change. This is important to note because the kinds of change which are informal may also be more likely to be temporary, and hence lost in decennial comparisons.

The Census Bureau data on other sources alone are not enough to allow us to measure the contribution of the informal sector to housing supply. Not surprisingly, CINCH, AHS and Census of Housing data do not identify illegal units. Other studies of informal sector housing help identify what kinds of additions or changes to dwellings are most likely to have informal sector characteristics, and show that at least some of the additions other than new construction were part of the informal sector.

9.   Interview with the author, October 1993.

10.   In a study combining several data sources, Hendershott and Smith used time series estimates of "net other additions" to the U.S. housing stock for 1961–85 to demonstrate that those additions—defined as additions to the housing stock other than new construction, less losses— play a major role in the short-run equilibration of the demand and supply for housing units. They estimate that "on average, a surge in household formation is half satisfied by reduced losses or non-new construction additions during the concurrent year" (1988: 366).

11.   The description of conversion and converters in Boston draws heavily on the work of Jacques Gordon (1987), who both developed and analyzed the BRA survey.

12.   Gellen argues that "illegal accessory apartment conversions in single-family zones" should be referred to as "nonconforming" uses rather than "illegal" units, appealing to the similarities between illegal accessory

apartments and the legal ones in the same or similar neighborhoods which predate the zoning codes under which they would otherwise be illegal (1987: 187).

13. Experience with legalization may vary. In a San Francisco study Gellen found that few owners of accessory apartments in San Francisco came forward to have illegal units legalized in 1980 when an amnesty was offered (1985: 188). He suggests that owners of illegal units preferred to keep their units secret to avoid paying the higher property taxes for rental property, as well as reducing reported income to the IRS. Owners are far more likely to report rental income for conventional apartments (86 percent) than for rented rooms (68 percent), accessory units (35 percent), or sublet lodgings (30 percent).

CHAPTER 4

Housing Alternatives for New Forms of Households

Sherry Ahrentzen

Introduction

During the past decade, architects, planners and developers have come up with new ideas for housing that can better meet household needs under the current conditions of social and demographic change. These new designs respond to a variety of new household forms (e.g., single-parent, multi-generational communities) as well as accommodate the desire for more flexible living space (e.g., homework; see chapter 5) and the need for greater affordability. Many of these designs include shared space as an important link between the social and physical aspects of housing. Unfortunately, these designs remain the exception rather than the rule. More common is for housing developers to downsize homes, making them more affordable but keeping conventional room arrangements intact. They simply shrink the floor plan proportionately rather than reconfiguring the rooms to allow for more flexibility, overlapping, and shared use. Thoughtful planning, siting, and design of housing can better accommodate many household types than do the traditional single-family detached home or the anonymous apartment complex. But such flexible and practical designs remain on the margin because of the housing market's emphasis on creating private, self-contained homes for independent nuclear families.

The widespread belief that promotes the singular, cultural ideal of the single-family home as the material manifestation of American rugged individualism and self-reliance denies our country's traditions and history of interdependent connections between extended families, neighbors, and communities. We must recognize that housing in America has been and should continue to be both a source of privacy and a source of sharing and community. Sensitive housing design can enhance both privacy and sharing, in homes and neighborhoods, so that the housing alternatives to the single-family detached house are neither a source of entrapment nor an emblem of second class status. Design can give residents more choices about interaction with others and thus a better sense of control, if not empowerment.

When we think about shared space in housing, or when people talk about neighboring or community, we all have somewhat amorphous ideas of what those concepts mean. I think this ambiguity is one of the reasons why we have a small number of well-developed housing communities that do enhance and support sharing. I have identified three general types of sharing that may help housing providers understand the ways in which design may enhance the positive and varied experience of sharing living space (see Table 9).

TABLE 9

Types of Sharing

Type	*Purpose*
Co-presence	Diminishes feelings of isolation
	Develops a sense of security; and facilitates security
	Establishes social identity
Affiliation (social-oriented interaction)	Companionship
	Social support
	Learning and growth
Instrumental (task-oriented interaction, or object exchange)	Increases the number of amenities one can have within financial limitations
	Eases the individual's time and efforts in domestic and child care responsibilities

We sometimes forget the importance of the presence of others in the spaces where we live. Though it is a passive form of sharing, the experience of people living daily lives in sight of each other often heightens our sense of security and diminishes feelings of isolation. This form of sharing, co-presence, becomes a basis for establishing a social identity. Affiliation, the second type of sharing, involves socially oriented interaction. Some households and communities desire this type of sharing as an opportunity to develop a social network among neighbors. Leisure Village, a subdivision outside San Diego, advertises itself as a place to develop friendships. The developers promote not only routine sociability, but the experience of affiliation with its promise of companionship and social support. Instrumental sharing, the third type, has two aspects. Households can increase their access to amenities, such as a workshop or specialized equipment, by sharing them with other households. Similarly, households can reduce domestic or child care tasks by sharing the time, effort, and responsibility with others.

Housing can be designed to inhibit, support, or passively contain each of these forms of sharing. Thoughtful and sensitive design can reduce impediments to desired sharing without undermining individual privacy. Common architectural and design elements—from the orientation of entry doors to the siting of buildings—can create intersections between home and neighborhood, and neighborhood and community, as well as enhancing different types of privacy (Sprague 1991).

Linking Private and Shared Space: The Concept of the Party Wall

For architect Jill Stoner, a wall does more than separate, it connects (Stoner 1989). Party walls both connect and separate units, and thus households, in a multi-unit complex. Through their design and construction, party walls can have different consequences.

Stoner demonstrates three ways to conceptually and architecturally treat the party wall. Thick and impenetrable walls signify that the people on either side of the wall are hostile, like the wall-building Yooks and Zooks in Dr. Seuss' The Butter Battle Book. Making the wall thin or transparent, like those between telephone booths, is a sign of neutrality and affords little more than symbolic privacy: it simply displays co-presence, a neutral point of sharing. Making the wall amenable to more direct sharing requires partial removal or readjustment of the separation to allow physical as well as visual access. Stoner solved this latter type in her designs for the New American House Competition (1984), and Harlem Infill Housing (1985–6). She expanded the party wall into a room between units, with doors from both adjoining units, enabling each household's privacy as well as social exchange and companionship.

This manipulation of the party wall to enhance and balance sharing and privacy in multi-units is also evident in housing designed by Dutch architect Herman Hertzberger in Kassel, Germany (Hertzberger 1986). He places well-lit alcoves off each stairwell landing that serves six families. The alcove provides a wonderful place for people to stop, sit and visit with others. Each unit also has a set of double doors at the entrance, off the stairwell. The inner door is glass, the outer door wood. Closing the outer door protects the privacy of the unit inhabitants. Opening the outer door enables residents to see stairwell users (and vice versa) through the glass inner door. A neutral "wall," the glass door blocks sound, but not sight. Parents can easily keep an eye on their children who play in the stairwell during the winter months.

In an Amsterdam housing project (Haarlemmer Houttuinen), Hertzberger designed connected balconies for adjoining apartment units. He separated each household's balcony with a two-level wall. Three-quarters of the wall is approximately seven feet high; while the remaining section near the edge of the balcony drops to about three feet. If residents want privacy they sit back from the edge shielded by the high wall. If they want to see or speak with their neighbors, they simply move closer to the edge. The choice is theirs.

Small elements like these that Stoner and Hertzberger provide enable residents to alternate and mix private and shared use of their living space in practical, simple ways. Designs can be more ambitious when patrons and residents are willing to treat sharing as an important and central aspect of residential life.

In the remainder of the chapter, I will describe a number of housing developments—primarily in the U.S.—that have been designed to allow for greater resident choice in the different forms of sharing mentioned previously.

Transitional Housing for Single Parent Families

About half of the single-parent households (overwhelmingly female-headed) in this country suffer some kind of housing problem: overcrowding, structural inadequacies, or rents that exceed half the household income. Low income is not the only serious constraint that many of these families face: many are leaving violent homes and other crisis situations. They may not have family nearby for security or support, or the family may already live in overcrowded conditions. Welfare hotels and emergency shelters prove severely inadequate as homes for these households. These families need a stable place in which to develop educational and job skills, or earn income sufficient to enter the private housing market.

In recent years, professionals, activists, and public officials have developed a new form of housing for these homeless families called transitional housing. Families who stay in this housing receive temporary (usually six months to two years) shelter, security, and services organized to facilitate their transition to some type of independent living. The construction of transitional shelters increased greatly with the availability of funds authorized by the 1987 Stuart B. McKinney Homeless Assistance Act. Unlike the bare bones emergency shelters that offer no privacy, transitional shelters often offer both private and shared space. The staff and residents can use the space to work together meeting not only basic needs for shelter, security, and food, but providing the knowledge, skills, and social support families need to become more self reliant. In the last decade, many transitional housing developments have been directed towards single-parent families.

Warren Village, Denver

Developed in Denver in 1974 (but based on an idea conceived in 1958), Warren Village is one of the oldest transitional housing complexes in the U.S. (Ahrentzen 1989; Sprague 1991). Worried that the project might fail as transitional housing, its financial backers initially limited the design to preclude the construction of shared spaces. They wanted to be sure the building could be inexpensively converted into conventional apartment units. Despite this handicap, the project has worked successfully as transitional housing for more than twenty years.

A seven-story masonry structure, Warren Village looks very much like a conventional apartment building. Its location across the street from expensive, high-rise condominiums demonstrates that transitional housing does not automatically produce negative effects on neighboring property values. The 96 units follow standard floor plans. Most are one- and two-bedroom; there are a few three-bedroom units. Social service programs, job training, job counselling, and child care are located in the basement. The job training programs have proven to be quite successful, to the point of attracting applicants from outside. Revenues from the services are used to subsidize housing costs.

An evaluation study conducted by ABT Associates ten years after Warren Village opened found that while slightly less than half (47 percent) of the household heads were employed when they entered the complex, nearly all (94 percent) were employed within two years after leaving. Reliance on welfare dropped from 65 percent of entering households to only six percent for the same households two years after their departure. Lack of a control group in this evaluation cautions us in assuming that it is the housing itself that has produced these positive changes in former residents' lives. But the changes are so large relative to the changes for the population of all welfare recipients that the experience with transitional shelter remains a likely, if not exclusive, reason for this improvement. Service providers were so convinced of the success of not simply providing shelter, but developing housing that enhances life skills and self-esteem, that they built another similar development, Decatur Place, which offers transitional housing for 100 households in a different section of Denver.

Women's' Advocate Housing, St. Paul

Women's Advocate Housing in St. Paul provides short-term transitional housing for single-parent families and single women (Sprague 1991). Most are fleeing violent homes. Initially started in a renovated older house in a single-family neighborhood, the demand quickly exceeded supply. The providers eventually purchased and renovated a neighboring house and built a connecting space between the two. The conversion to transitional housing and the connecting space, used as a shared lounge area, is not distinguishable from the smaller-scale residences in the neighborhood. The ground floor includes a conference center, children's play room, staff office, and kitchen (with shared kitchen arrangements); the upper floor includes the bedrooms.

Vision Teen Parent Home, Cape Cod

Some transitional housing targets teen mothers (Sprague 1991). Not only do homeless teen mothers face the responsibilities of parenting as adolescents, many lack a high school education (and subsequent access to decent-paying jobs). Some are evicted from their parents' homes once they become pregnant. A transitional housing project for teen mothers in Cape Cod employs different degrees of sharing and privacy to match the teens' needs for both support and independence. The architects paid special attention to the advice of service providers and teen mothers when they designed the mix of private and shared spaces. Some teen mothers share a dwelling unit with four other mothers. Each family has a bedroom for mother and child, while all share a common kitchen and dining area. Mothers who are more independent live in one bedroom suites with a kitchen, bath, and bedroom. Once a week all the residents share a meal in the large shared kitchen and dining area on the first floor. Integral to the project is the opportunity for the teen mothers to increase their independence while continuing to experience community support.

Vacant Lots Project Proposal, New York City

New York City architect Conrad Levenson proposed a design for a large transitional housing development that placed social service programs on the ground floor (an adolescent recreation center, child care center, and counselling offices) and residential units on the upper floors (Ahrentzen 1989). However, Levenson went further than most in his proposal for residential spaces by acknowledging the diversity of single-parent households. Some families need considerable space, some want a great deal of sharing, others want different types of sharing at different times, and so forth. His design accommodates this diversity in a way that is straightforward and relatively inexpensive by incorporating "swing rooms." Located between two two-bedroom dwelling units, the swing rooms are flexible spaces that can be used as a shared lounge and dining area between the two households; or the swing room can be used as a private third bedroom for a large household that needs the extra space. Since families often add and lose members as they grow, swing rooms accommodate these changes. Unfortunately, the project was never built.

Willowbrook Green, Los Angeles

Willowbrook Green in the Watts area of Los Angeles began as transitional housing but eventually became permanent housing for low-income single parents (Ahrentzen 1989). Dolores Hayden's pathbreaking book Redesigning the American Dream, advocating varieties of shared housing in suburban neighborhoods, inspired a member of the Los Angeles city council to appropriate public revenue for the kind of project Hayden had described in her book. Architect Ena Dubnoff designed the development. She took particular care to combine private and shared space and to use architectural forms, such as peaked roofs, to establish a sense of residential identity to the place. The self-contained dwelling units are built around a child care center for the residents, 80 percent of whom are single mothers. The site is near Martin King Luther Hospital, not only ensuring easier access to medical care, but near a major employment center for low- and semi-skilled workers.

Cohousing

Cohousing is an American term for a type of shared housing development that began as a grass roots movement in Denmark and Holland in the 1970s. The developments include self-contained housing units for each family along with shared communal facilities, and so offer the advantages of both privacy and sharing. The Danes call them "bofaelleskaber," the Dutch "central woheen." There are about 90 cohousing developments in Denmark (which has the population size of the state of Wisconsin) and 55 in Holland, with many more under construction.

Cohousing possesses four qualities that set it apart from more conventional planned unit developments (McCamant and Durrett 1988). First, future residents plan the housing complex together and participate in all stages of development. They pool their funds, hire the architects, obtain financing, and so forth. Second, once built, the residents manage the project together rather than hiring a professional management staff.

They share not only the physical maintenance tasks, but the organization and provision of a variety of social and domestic activities such as shared meals, child care, recreational events, celebrations and so forth. Third, cohousing is intentionally designed to enhance neighboring and a community atmosphere. (About three out of four cohousing residents I interviewed in Denmark and Holland joined cohousing in order to live in a community where they and their children could play with and talk to their neighbors.) Kathryn McCamant and Charles Durrett, two of the cohousing pioneers in the U.S., write in their book Cohousing about the cohousing resident who complained jokingly that after parking his car in the lot near his home, it took him 45 minutes and two beers to reach his doorstep because he talks to so many neighbors along the way. Finally, cohousing includes shared facilities that are used for daily activities: eating in a common dining area, watching children, cleaning up after meals, and so forth. Most developments include a centrally located common house with a large kitchen and dining room. Depending on the size and interest of the community, there can be other common spaces in adjoining rooms or in nearby buildings: child care facilities, office space, repair, or machine shops.

Each household lives in a self-contained unit with its own kitchen, bath, living room, and bedrooms. Residents routinely fix breakfast and lunch in their units, but usually eat dinner together in the community dining room. Sharing meals together varies among different cohousing communities. Some eat together as few as three nights a week, while others eat together every night. While the residents who live in cohousing communities enjoy preparing and eating the common meal, the private kitchens allow them the choice to eat privately whenever they wish.

Residents usually take turns planning and preparing meals for others. Some have very formal programs, when days and tasks are assigned a month in advance. Others, especially those small groups in which the people get to know each other well over time, work much more informally. They may simply indicate each morning (on a community bulletin board) whether or not they plan to eat a shared meal that evening. It is similar to how a family might operate, especially one with teen-aged children who are unlikely to provide a one-week or 24-hour notice of whether or not they'll be at dinner. In large communities with sixty households, for example, four households working together to provide the evening meal would need to do so only twice a month (assuming shared meals every night of the week). The four households work hard two nights a month in return for 28 evenings with meal service provided by their neighbors.

Scale is an important issue in cohousing. Developments with more than thirty households can sometimes lose the sense of community that residents hope to experience as they share space, tasks, and responsibilities with others. The Dutch handle this problem by breaking down the common spaces in cohousing developments into smaller facilities that six to eight households share. One 35-unit community then might have five or six common houses. In contrast, the Danes usually have one large common house regardless of the size of the development.

Shared facilities can take many forms and styles as do the cohousing developments themselves. Dwellings may be organized in blocks, around courtyards, or along interior streets. Sometimes projects consist of a conglomeration of single-family homes. The more dense projects trade private for community space. However, in these cases residents manipulate home interiors to maximize the usable area.

Cohousing in Europe appeals to a variety of household types. Cohousing residents in Holland are single persons (47 percent) and single parents (28 percent). Fewer than one in four resident households are couples with children (16 percent) or without (7 percent). Danish cohousers, who mainly own their units, consist largely of married couples with children (45 percent) and single parent families (29 percent). A small portion of residents are single (16 percent) or couples without children (one percent).

Aarhus, Denmark

In Aarhus, Denmark, cohousing residents wanted to create a physical landmark to distinguish their community. The architect and residents came up with the idea of a tower. They made the symbolic structure practical by creating three studio apartments in the upper floors. These were originally intended to house adolescents on a temporary basis, so that teenagers seeking respite from their parents could live apart for awhile without leaving the larger community. Also, the studios are used by couples having marital or partnership problems to temporarily separate, with one partner moving into the tower studio and the other remaining in the dwelling. These extra rooms enable community residents to obtain a degree of private space that would be difficult to obtain in a more conventional housing situation. The close location of these spaces allow residents to separate from some, but not all the members of the larger community.

Waginenen, Holland

The cohousing development in Waginenen, Holland is especially diverse. One section of the development consists of several townhouses. The townhouse residents use their own kitchens and do not share meals, using the common house primarily as a meeting and exercise area. They enjoy the security of the community (i.e., co-presence) but with a minimum of shared responsibility. Another section of the development includes two- and three- bedroom apartments, each with a private kitchen. However, these residents share dinner three to five times a week with the four or five other households sharing the same stairwell area. Each stairwell group has a shared kitchen/lounge area on the first floor. The final section of the development, in a single building, houses four or five residents, mainly single, who each possess his/her own bedroom, but share a living room, bathroom, and a large kitchen with regular common meals. This one cohousing community successfully integrates different layers of sharing and privacy.

For the entire complex there is a shared community center with a multipurpose room and a community garden. Other community amenities are guest rooms. Residents do not need to maintain an extra bedroom in their own unit in order to provide for the occasional family, friend, or visiting professor who stays with them. Having bedrooms and washrooms for guests in one of the buildings of the complex provides residents further control over their privacy while enhancing the opportunity to share with visitors.

Cohousing in the United States

In late 1992, there were about thirty cohousing projects at various stages of planning and development in the U.S. Three were completed and occupied: one outside Seattle, another outside Boulder, Colorado, and the third in Davis, California. Resident participation makes for a minimum two year development process, but usually at least twice as long before the development is constructed and occupied.

The cohousing development on Bainbridge Island near Seattle, Washington is composed of duplexes with a common house. This project took only eighteen months from initial plan to construction, but the middle-class residents included two architects and a couple of engineers who used their skills to speed up the process. Only the Davis project provides for some moderate-income households. Organizers for a Sacramento project hope to have 20 percent moderate and 20 percent low-income households. Organizers for a project in Aspen have asked the local municipal government to subsidize a portion of the project units for low-income households. Because it does not involve new construction, the Davis cohousing development is less expensive.

The State of Wisconsin funded research studying the economic and siting feasibility of cohousing for low income single-parent families. Part of the study involved determining whether or not these families were interested in cohousing arrangements (see Garber 1991). Interviews with such family heads produced mixed results. Some found the idea appealing, some liked the idea and wanted it right away, and others rejected the idea altogether. Those women who had experienced privacy and security at home and who had a greater sense of control of their lives had a greater desire to share with others some of the amenities of cohousing. But for women who had never been able to have any privacy in their residences, the idea that they would always have to be sharing was not appealing. Ideas for combining privacy and sharing must be considered in terms of people's sense of control over their lives and their living spaces. Cohousing may work for some low income households, as well as moderate income and middle income households, but like any form of housing, it is not the ideal solution for everyone.

Shared Housing

Shared housing refers to situations in which two or more families or individuals live together in one unit or house. Usually each adult has a private bedroom and bath, and shares the remaining rooms in common. There are many shared housing units in the United States. (See chapter 3 for more on the shared housing stock.) A recent study of shared housing units in Milwaukee and Chicago (Despres 1991) found that the arrangement worked well with many of the old townhouses originally designed to shelter servants. The builders had constructed the units for two households: servants and owners. The corridor and room placement nicely balances private and shared space for contemporary sharing. But much of the existing housing stock does not support these shared arrangements.

Architect Ted Smith designed shared housing from scratch in the suburban beach-front community of Del Mar, California (Franck 1989). The attractive GoHomes he created provide one kitchen shared among four residents, each with their own two-room unit. His design met the zoning ordinance in a way that not only produced beautiful structures, but flexible and relatively affordable space for the few residents. So far he has built three projects. The units in succeeding GoHome developments get larger, allowing both more private and shared space.

Accessory apartments are usually built as an addition to an existing single-family structure, but also may be converted from existing rooms. In either case, the accessory apartment houses another household. As Hardman discusses in greater detail in chapter 3, these units are built for numerous reasons: prospects of rental income or housing for family or friends. The Double Unit Opportunity (DUO) program was established in San Francisco to help create more accessory apartments and accessory units. The non-profit organization provides free counselling, information services, preliminary architectural designs, and financial resources to home owners who want to convert part of their homes into accessory units for families. Participation in the program requires that the accessory units be rented to low income or moderate income households. Research on DUO projects found that conversion was one-third to one-quarter the cost of new construction for comparable units. As a result, owners could charge rents anywhere from $100 to $150 less per month. Forty-two percent of the DUO clients were single mothers seeking supplemental income. The accessory unit additions offered affordable units in a tight housing market, and improved the financial security of economically vulnerable households.

Hybrid Housing

Hybrid housing is designed to combine business and residence spaces and activity under the management and occupancy of residents (Ahrentzen 1991). Many hybrid houses have been developed for wealthy households, but some architects have begun to design housing for low and moderate income households that will enable residents to put their residential space to economic use. Jacqueline Leavitt discusses one such effort in chapter 5. Proper design ensures that domestic and business activities do not compete against each other, but work with each other.

The Electric Art Block in Santa Monica, California provides moderate income artisans the opportunity to work in their homes. South Prescott Village, in Oakland, also serves low income artists who live in their studios. Residents in these two hybrid settings claim that their home now pays for itself in many ways. For instance, residents can count a portion of their rents as tax deductible business expenses.

The hybrid idea is not new. A traditional image of home-based workplaces is the house-over-the-shop on the main street in the frontier town. Small towns and old urban neighborhoods still have many buildings along main streets or commercial arterials with residential units above commercial establishments. Outlawed by many zoning ordinances, these combinations are now finding their way back into mixed-use zones as hybrid housing. For instance, in Oak Creek, Wisconsin a 40-unit building was constructed as a mixed-use hybrid arrangement. The residents live upstairs and conduct business in their shops and services on the ground floor: dentists, lawyers, and retailers. The residents expressed satisfaction with the available amenities and the security they felt with the continuing presence of their neighbors who shared a similar economic and social investment in the community.

Conclusion

The myth of the importance of the single-family home as exclusively desirable housing restricts opportunities to design and develop more housing alternatives. The images of such single-family living promoted by advertisers, developers, and bankers powerfully affects our ideas about what family life should be. We must become more knowledgeable about the actual nature of U.S. households and how they want to live rather than perpetuating the myths that restrict our choices. Architects and planners especially need to consider ways of enhancing the prospects for shared housing so that more people will perceive its viability as a desirable housing alternative instead of as a demeaning and stigmatizing situation.

The various types of shared housing described in this chapter present different ways and degrees of sharing: living and business space, housing amenities, work and domestic activities, and so forth. Equally important is the purpose and intent behind these sharing arrangements. The demographic characteristics of households have changed significantly over the past three or four decades. Drastic changes have also occurred in the means of support for households, particularly for smaller families with marginal economic security. Social and economic ties now rely on telecommunications, elaborate transportation systems, and commercial and institutional supports more than small community networks, extended families living in close proximity, and collective work groups such as trade unions. Because all households do not have equal access to these more institutional resources, many become further disadvantaged and less in control of their lives and opportunities. We must develop our physical infrastructure—housing and neighborhoods—to enrich and support those social networks that can support myriad families and households in practical, flexible, and affordable ways.

CHAPTER 5

DESIGNING WOMEN'S WELFARE: HOME/WORK

Jacqueline Leavitt

Home economists at the turn of the century referred to the house as the factory for women's labor, as a place where housework conformed to a set of standards. Over the course of the twentieth century women from all races and ethnicities, including middle-class housewives, left the house to find paid labor. Today, widespread economic restructuring has accelerated this trend, producing a wider variety of specialized labor markets for women. Among these shifting employment relations, what role does the house play as a site for paid labor for women?[1]

Answering this question requires a close look at what some analysts refer to as domestic architecture (Wright 1981), and by extension the design of the surrounding neighborhood, which might be referred to as domestic planning. Much of women's work is carried out in both places. The design of both occurs through a mix of social and political activity. Home and neighborhood are places where women struggle with and resist the dominance of real estate pressures and financial interests (Pickvance 1976). The viability of home-based work in today's era of economic turmoil and reshaping brings domestic architecture and domestic planning to the forefront of the debate about the nature of wage work.

The pull or tension between women working either in the home or at a separate place of employment has historical roots traceable to the colonial period. Rural women migrated to the cities and filled jobs formerly held by men who died during the War for Independence. These single women usually lived together under one roof in a building called the "manufactory". Manufacturers of wool and cloth obtained factory permits claiming they would employ otherwise useless and burdensome women and children. The manufactory was an alternative to the workhouse for poor widows and their dependents, but hardly an ideal environment for young women. It offered no time "for maternal duties" and the tasks required by manufacturers seldom matched the interests of the women employees (Abramovitz 1988: 89–90; Kessler-Harris 1982: 7, 17).

Throughout the nineteenth century class distinctions among women sharpened (Stansell 1987). Early in the century spinning bees were held on the Boston Common encouraging women of middle and lower class standing to continue spinning in their home. Other women continued to practice midwifery and nursing from their home bases. But as early as 1814 textile work was consolidated in mills, and "only the middling and better sort could afford the version of domesticity that was separate from family income production" (Evans 1989: 62). For some women, mothering and breadwinning remained one and the same thing even if "the home did lose its status as the center of production" (Daniels 1989: 18, 21–22).

African-American women in the late nineteenth and early twentieth century were excluded from factory work (Harley 1990: 336–349). Although middle-class African-American women found status working as community volunteers, a higher proportion of African-American women than white women worked in paid occupations such as beauty parlor operators, seamstresses, launderers, sharecroppers, and boarding house managers (Boris 1989: 33-52). In the 1890 census, women in paid occupations outside the house were largely young, single, transplants from American farms, and immigrants from Europe. Working immigrant wives in New England and African-American married women in the South were the exception (Scharf 1980).

By the 1920s, women moved into white collar jobs and soon dominated elementary teaching, nursing, social work, librarianship, clerical, and sales. A startling shift occurred in the demographic profile. "Native white women of native parentage accounted for the largest percentage of the growth." (Scharf 1980: 11). As these women entered the labor force from the growing middle class, public concern about poor and dangerous working conditions gained more attention than it had during earlier periods when working class and minority women had entered the labor force. Married women who worked usually took unskilled and semi-skilled factory jobs or did laundry at home or elsewhere. By 1930 married women made up about 29 percent of the work force, an increase of six percent from a decade earlier (Kessler-Harris 1982: 227).

High unemployment during 1930s made way for the revival of earlier arguments about the necessity of keeping women at home and out of the labor market. As a result, the social profile of the female labor force shifted. Working women at the end of the decade tended to be married, older, and better educated than wage-earning women in the late 1920s (Kessler-Harris 1982: 231, 254). Many worked out of their homes. The Women's Bureau identified industrial outworking in the house in 1937 for a variety of products: stringing toys, carding buttons, sewing on hooks and eyes, making bobby pins, safety pins, garters, lamp shades, paper boxes and bags, shelling nuts, addressing envelopes, hooking rugs, knitting, crocheting, embroidering, decorating postcards, and working on cheap jewelry. Doing such piecework in the home was widely condemned. President Roosevelt issued an executive order requiring employers to pay homebound workers (e.g., handicapped people, caretakers for an invalid) factory rate wages (Kessler-Harris 1982: 269-70). But such regulations did not cover women who were self-supporting, those who contributed to their households such as an extended family, or those who were married with children.

During the Second World War a larger proportion of women entered the labor force to replace the loss of male labor to the military. Popular belief has it that this arrangement was temporary and unpopular among women, most of whom willingly returned to the bosom of the nuclear family after the war. However, as early as 1950, more white married women in upper income households were working full-time than ever before. Women of all sorts entered the labor market during the 1950s, although many worked part-time. "In 1960, 39 percent of married women living with their husbands and with children between the ages of 6 and 17 were working, compared to 26 percent in 1948." (Gatlin 1987: 30) Mothers of pre-school-age children also increased their workforce participation rate, from 10.7 percent in 1948 to 18.6 percent in 1960.

As women continued to enter the work force, they were concentrated in female-dominated occupations, as health care aides and technicians, beauticians, waitresses, office cleaning ladies, and clerical workers. These jobs were attractive because of the compatibility with women's responsibilities as mothers and wives. African-American women were hired when certain occupations faced increasing shortages of labor, although they were more vulnerable than white women to layoffs. More women were working during the 1950s than conventional belief recognizes.

These substantial participation rates were overshadowed by the rapid growth in women's labor force participation rate since the early 1960s (Rix 1987: 1988). Unfortunately these new women employees work at occupations that pay poorly relative to the occupations dominated by males: secretaries, nurses, teachers, and service workers (Blank 1988: 69). Since women are more likely to work part-time than men, they receive lower wages, fewer fringe benefits, and little future advancement.

Homework and Our Changing Economy

Current economic conditions continue to encourage the employment of women, but often do little to improve their economic power and choice. The expansion of the global economy has increased entry barriers to the declining share of high wage jobs in the formal sector of the economy, while expanding low wage jobs in the rapidly growing informal sector (Bluestone and Harrison 1982; Feagin and Smith 1987). For instance, unionized textile factories in one region of the country shut down, eventually replaced with small-scale sweat shops in another. Seeking to shift the burden of economic uncertainty, firms encourage piecework or contract with self-employed workers, many of whom work at home. The self employed enjoy greater status than the pieceworker, but not nearly as much independence as believed. Most self-employed people contract with corporations. The corporations find this arrangement attractive since they need not offer training, facilities, or benefits to the contractor as they frequently must for employees (Rubery 1988).

The economic uncertainty fostered by the uneven consequences of restructuring has encouraged many more households to combine wage labor and home based work to obtain more income and better use existing resources (Pahl 1984: 1988). Women make up the fastest growing portion of this self-employed work force (Christopherson 1989; Haber, Lamas and Lichtenstein 1987: 17-23). But they do so as independent clerical contractors rather than professional advisors. Thousands of such home-based contractors were participating in pilot programs for such companies as New York Telephone, American Express, Walgreens, Investors Diversified Services, and Blue Cross-Blue Shield in the late 1980s (Christopherson 1989: 136–137). Insurance industry firms were conducting similar experiments as well.

> Although still rare, insurance companies are beginning to experiment with telecommuting, or homework. The motivation is both cost reduction and the desire to attract or retain the preferred work force—educated, preferably married, and usually white women. (Baran 1988: 693)

One company hired one-sixth of its claims adjustors as independent piece-rate contractors using home computers electronically linked to the company's mainframe.

Working at home has increased.[2] An estimated 1.9 million individuals (two-thirds women) reported that their home was their exclusive place of work in the mid 1980s.[3] (Christopherson 1989: 131–14; Rubery 1988: 265). A nationwide survey conducted in 1989 estimated that 6.7 million out of

26.6 million full-time workers work at home (Ahrentzen 1992). The United States Chamber of Commerce estimates that 11 million worked out of their home in 1990. The vast majority of these home workers are women. Despite the economic burdens of many forms of home based work, the shift does offer advantages and opportunities, especially for women. Feelings of security and safety increase for women no longer subjected to male domination in workplace environments. Many home-based working women enjoy more control over their time. They can leave the house to conduct errands, meet clients, and exercise. They can and do organize the relationship between domestic and work space to protect against the encroachment of the demands of work on the domestic sphere (Ahrentzen 1992).

In her study of clerical and manufacturing home workers, Lozano found that women valued their escape from the indignities of "patriarchal authority, gender stereotyping, and . . . occupational elitism" (1989: 109). Working at home insulates women from stereotypical and demeaning remarks; for instance, male supervisors who associate particular tasks with gender roles or who claim that women can withstand greater repetitive tasks because they can endure the pain of childbirth.[4] In a study of female Mexican piece workers, Roldan (despite her skepticism) found that many reported increased feelings of esteem because they could contribute to household earnings without neglecting domestic responsibilities (Roldan 1985). Similar research found that among Cuban households in Miami, home work was a strategy for maximizing earnings and reconciling cultural and economic demands (Fernandez-Kelly and Garcia 1989).

Home work may be preferable for many women who measure its worth not simply by economic remuneration but also by improved self-esteem and assertiveness against gender discrimination, as well as by increasing positive identification with the house (Matthews 1987). However, home-work may not seriously challenge male privilege, instead offering a resourceful, if limited accommodation (Leidner 1988: 69–94). In the short run, to cope with economic adversity individual households will continue to devise ways that include home work. Women play a central role in these efforts and so change the meaning and use of home space. Housing developers, real estate brokers, and builders have found women's labor market participation a useful marketing device in today's economy. Allen and Wolkowitz write:

> The seminars and conferences being organized to press for the relaxation of planning regulations in residential areas, or the adaptation of domestic housing for home-based production, seem a transparent effort to present an image of homeworking as an acceptable alternative. (1987: 63)

Accommodating Home Work

Some of the earliest New England dwellings combined work space and living space. Many seventeenth century town dwellers lived in tiny one room halls that sheltered all household activities: work, cooking, eating, and sleeping. New England farmers developed the "continuous house" which combined stables, shed, and dwelling under a single roof (Foley 1980: 14, 20). But such household mixing gave way to more organized forms of specialization and segregation of use with the spread of industrialization.

For instance, although a few New York City tenements combined dwelling units to provide a kindergarten for the children of women working outside the home (Hayden 1984), work was accommodated within the existing buildings. Regulations, more than design, were influential during this period. In 1893, the first licensing law was passed to control the sanitary conditions for home work. The tenement owner was required to give written consent to allow the building to be used for home work, while the piece work employers had to obtain licenses. The Women's City Club and The City Club of New York opposed the official approval and licensing of homework, claiming that the understaffed regulatory agency (25 inspectors overseeing 16,000 licensed tenements) could not possibly ensure security for the home workers (The Women's City Club 1920). The rules simply legitimized an exploitative situation. Nineteenth century home work was not limited to the working class. Doctors and dentists, for example, frequently combined workplace and home. Some manufacturers had warehouses behind their homes. But even for these upscale users the home work space was not the product of purposeful physical design, but primarily accommodation to existing forms (Burnett 1986).

The house continues to be used to improve economic security through sharing domestic and income-generating space. Pratt and Hanson have studied how working-class households in Worcester, Massachusetts used housing to improve their economic security. The inheritance of a triple-decker, freestanding, wood-frame house enables young families to either rent from relatives or live rent-free. This subsidy not only tied the new families to the neighborhood, but reduced the reliance on wage work (1991: 71). Women in a Cuban enclave in Miami convert the covered porches of their houses into sewing shops and hire neighbors (Fernandez-Kelly and Garcia 1989: 176).

Designing Spaces for Homework

Designing the home as both work space and domestic space emerged in the 1980s, inspired by the entry of a larger proportion of married women with small children into the labor market, women for whom home work might prove especially appropriate (Bianchi and Spain 1986). Many analysts argued that dwellings could be designed and constructed that would better meet the needs of single-parent households by reducing child care, transportation and energy costs (Leavitt 1990). These ideas usually include rental rooms, offices, and other work space.

Households providing informal nursing care for kin frequently adapt the physical structure to meet the needs of the dependent member and the (usually female) caretaker. Increasingly, designers are taking these needs into account as they allow for wheelchair access, visual access to outdoor scenes through lower window heights, and skylights. Whether as paid or unpaid caretakers, women would benefit from such improvements (Finch and Groves 1983).

Ahrentzen has conducted research to codify design guidelines for work in the house. She interviewed homeworkers to identify the benefits and costs they face in adapting their house to accommodate paid work (Ahrentzen 1987). Most proceeded on an ad hoc basis, ranging from clearing space on an existing table surface to building an additional freestanding workplace. Poor contemporary homeworkers, like their predecessors, make the same space serve multiple purposes: the garment worker uses a kitchen table to sew. In contrast, middle-class professionals or artists are more likely (and able) to physically remodel rooms and garages to provide specialized work spaces. Purposefully designed professional workspace includes the GoHome in Del Mar, California which has shared kitchens with private entrances and shared office spaces and workshops as well (Franck 1989; see chapter 4).

Designs for home offices proliferated with the widespread availability of personal computers. But the designs tended to focus on the needs of two-income households, offering the middle-class woman an environment that would facilitate working in the home on a regular basis. Gurstein (1990) interviewed home and office workers and used their experience and ideas to formulate design recommendations. For instance, work in the home should be separated physically from the other rooms, such as by using separate entrances. At the neighborhood level, Gurstein recommends common work centers within walking distance of the users. When people live near their workplace, they spend less time commuting and so have more time and flexibility for participating in domestic and public life. Furthermore, the convenience of proximity enables workers to more easily iron out extended family ties and reciprocal family relations without jeopardizing their work. Purposefully designed home and neighborhood arrangements that facilitate such cohesive community life suggest a contemporary benefit of homework.

Design Examples for Different Income Groups

In the mid- to late 1980s, the New American House competition called for a design that integrated space for wage and domestic work in the same house. Inspired by Alvin Toffler's (1980) image of the "electronic cottage", the New American House program sponsors solicited designs for what they hoped would be a practical and affordable prototype in a cluster of six units. The program's announcement read:

> The intent of this competition is to generate and disseminate innovative concepts for the design of urban housing units which will accurately reflect the needs of non-traditional, professional households [defined as single-parent families, two-income families, unrelated young adults sharing a single residence, adults without children at home and retired, active adults . . .] (Leavitt 1989: 170).

The six units could be grouped into combinations of two and four, three and three or six row houses. Although the units had to be identical, they could be rotated or flipped to provide mirror images. The winning design by Troy West and myself presented six row house units. The street facing included the more public workplace side for each unit (workplace or work space refers to an area for paid work). The work spaces (199 square feet each) accommodated such uses as an artist's studio, a lawyer's office, and child care center.

Building the plan proved more difficult than anticipated. Neighbors resisted the original appearance and the zoning commission resisted efforts to reduce the number of parking spaces per unit; the original land purchase agreements fell through (Franck and Ahrentzen 1989; Birch 1985). Potential investors balked at the idea of providing a specific place for wage work in a residential town house. Others doubted that rowhouses in the city could compete with single-family detached houses in the suburban areas. Common spaces and uses like the child care center in the original design were dropped. The scheme proved much more difficult to implement than the original competition program had promised.[5]

Even if the houses had been built as planned, the $70,000 price would have eliminated low income single parent families without subsidies. A recent design addressed this problem head on. Progressive Architecture sponsored an architectural design competition for an affordable single-family house on a site in Cleveland, Ohio. Judith Sheine and I developed a design using ideas collected from a MS. magazine survey of women's housing and neighborhood needs (Leavitt and Saegert 1984). The entry, "The Double Dream", combined two single family attached houses using a variety of flexible spaces. The accompanying scenarios described how the design facilitated homework:

Karen, through her university classes, became friendly with Gail, the departmental secretary. Gail, a single mother with a two year old girl and Carol, another single mother of a nine-year-old girl, have been househunting together. Gail and Carol want to rent one house. They have talked about each of them using the entire lower or second level for bedrooms for themselves and their child . . . Gail and Carol prefer rearranging the upstairs bedrooms in order that the younger one has a sleep-in nook, separated from the nine-year-old's, and that Carol use the lower level. Carol, a sales representative for a leading clothing company, primarily works out of the house, leaving her available for partial child care (Sheine and Leavitt 1991).

While this design may be appropriate for middle-income residents, it does not address the housing needs of low income minority women, especially those in public housing. How might the purposeful integration of work and domestic space improve the economic viability of public housing, while enhancing resident control of their residential environment?

Homework and Public Housing

Nickerson Gardens, one of twenty-one city public housing projects in Los Angeles, is the largest public housing project west of the Mississippi (1,066 units in 154 predominantly two-story buildings on 68 acres). Nickerson Gardens houses about 4,900 people, of whom 2,000 are children.[6] The population is primarily African-American, although in the last few years about 600 Latino and Chicano families have moved there. Public housing represents a great economic resource for this low income population, 84 percent of whose adults were unemployed in June of 1992.

A 1988 resident self-survey of their interests, skills, and support needs found that many adults had experience in service and clerical jobs. Most respondents wanted to work as administrative support (especially with computers) and as nurses and physician assistants. Underutilized skills that could lend themselves to homework included: cooking, child care, typing, auto mechanics, sewing clothes, crocheting, knitting, hair styling, clerical, and secretarial work. Residents have continuously avoided wage labor that would threaten reduction of public aid without substantially improving household income. But informal economic activity does occur in important, if modest ways. Residents supply a can of soda to a neighbor, babysit or braid hair, all for small fees. Recent changes in housing authority regulations now encourage entrepreneurialism. One resident has been allowed to operate a kiosk beside his unit where he sells sodas and candies. Hand-crafted earrings and candy are sold at a resident council office on site.

How can public housing units like those at Nickerson be adapted to accommodate paid work? Currently some two story and a few one story units have been converted into office space, including conference rooms, usually with the kitchens retained. In two cases, walls of adjoining units were partially demolished to create connecting doors. The row house configuration of Nickerson lends itself to other more extensive remodelling that could provide exclusive space for paid work. Additions to both the front and back could be completely or partially enclosed in ways to expand the front porch or add space to the dining room. This model has been used in row housing in Guadalajara, Mexico, where residents have added small cafes, convenience stores, and balconies. Such modest renovations could make dramatic improvements to the appearance of the projects by breaking up the repetitive institutional pattern of public housing. Neighborhood employment centers could be set up by converting an entire row of residential units into workplaces. Child care facilities, food cooperatives, restaurant and bakery facilities, and various small manufacturing spaces could be planned and designed for these spaces.[7]

Conclusion

Intersecting research about economic restructuring, design, and gender calls for going beyond merely romanticizing the closer social relations that are possible at home, or rejecting home-based work because of arguments invoked about such complex issues as unionization or male privilege. The economic benefits of home work assert its viability as a constructive response to current economic restructuring. Domestic architecture based on economical use of the house often implies innovative designs and adaptations that combine use of residential and work space. Thoughtful design of home work space can keep work requirements from impinging on domestic space and activities or negatively impacting the surrounding neighborhood. Domestic planning that prioritizes constructive response to neighborhood residents' needs and skills over physical separation of social and economic uses holds promise for creating more cohesive communities.

Further legitimating paid work in the house can be a positive aspect of community development particularly when proper protections for home workers are in place. Improvements in the current home work situation could include overhead allowances, inclusion of home workers in health and safety regulations and relaxation of planning regulations that apply the same restrictions to home working as to separate business establishments (Allen and Wolkowitz 1987: 190–200). The context for home work must be analyzed case by case. For example, encouraging homework in housing developments with high unemployment should not be seen as an end in itself. There needs to be an understanding of the larger economic trends the residents face and of the limited employment alternatives available.

Many designers have developed proposals and projects for women that break from the conventional use of residential dwellings as exclusively domestic space. The efforts to combine work space with domestic space, especially for low income female-headed households, are part of a much larger effort to change longstanding gender prejudices and practices that disadvantage women in their use of all kinds of residential space (Sprague 1991; Roberts 1991; Thiberg 1990; Franck and Ahrentzen 1989; Hayden 1984; Matrix 1984; Keller 1981; Wright 1981; Wekerle et. al. 1980). Related literature covers issues of access, influence, land use policy, zoning, and mobility (Little, Peake and Richardson 1988; McClain with Doyle 1984; Keller 1981; Ritzdorf 1986). Though an important component of domestic architecture and domestic planning, home work hardly threatens to undermine the conventional separation of work and residence, but it does offer an important and useful alternative for households not well-served by existing arrangements.

Notes

1. Although the production and use of the built environment is part of the research project in critical urbanism (Harvey 1985; Soja 1989; Goodchild 6:131–144) and linkages are also being made between feminist theory and geography and sociology (Pratt and Hanson 15:55–74; Drewes Nielsen 15:42–54; Wekerle and Rutherford 1989), further extension, particularly to domestic design and differences among women, has rarely been touched upon.

2. For a smaller and undetermined number of people, the house itself has become the place of paid and unpaid work. Rather than bringing work into the house, certain types of work and house are interchangeable. The leading examples are live-in workers at shelters for the homeless, or residents who manage housing from an on-site office and/or their unit. Without the existence of the house or shelter, no work would exist. But even for those workers, the house has not been designed as a workspace for wage labor.

3. Self-employment has grown in the 1980s, particularly in the service sictor. Part-time work has also been growing an is the most prevalent of flexible jobs, but temporary work has also been increasing. In the United States, at least three million people work as temporaries and some companies have their own temporary labor services.

4. The factory "harem" is a particularly graphic image of negative social relations, described by M. Patricia Fernandez-Kelly (Lozano 1989: 110). Lozano points out that men may be subjected to similar types of authority, "But the bases of this control differ for men and women" (Lozano 1989: 113).

5. This one-stage competition was announced in 1984, although planning for it had begun two years earlier.

6. Figures vary. June 1992 statistics from the Housing Authority report a total of 3,689 people of which 1,852 were 13 years and under.

7. The integration of cottage industry in economic strategies and its visibility in the build environment in Third World countries is far more obvious and refined an intervention than is the informal economy in the First World (Strassman 1985; Moser and Peake 1987). Currently, the types of jobs that are generally being provided for public housing residents close to home are relatively few—arising from on-site service agencies, temporary work with the Housing Authority itself, and longer range jobs from a few who participate in resident management.

CHAPTER 6

Lakefront SRO Corporation:
Reviving Single Room Occupancy Housing

Jean Butzen

While there are positive developments in the struggle to preserve all of Chicago's remaining single-room occupancy (SRO) housing stock, attempts by nonprofit organizations to develop their own brand of SRO housing is distinct in many ways from what the private market is doing. Nonprofit housing is by far the smallest segment of the SRO housing market right now, but it is an area that is growing rapidly in Chicago. It has been in existence throughout the country since the late 1970s.

After describing the range of types of SRO housing, a broad historical summary of single-room-occupancy housing, from the early part of the century to where we are today, will be presented. Lakefront SRO Corporation's nonprofit development model for SRO housing in Chicago will then be covered. I will discuss the financing and acquisition of buildings, property management, and social service delivery systems, and then end with some information on the politics of the SRO housing industry.

What Is SRO Housing?

"Single-room-occupancy" is a bureaucratic term created to define a type of housing that resists definition. Someone once said to me, "Nobody knows what an SRO is, and yet everybody knows what it is." It's the place where we visited an elderly relative, and the residence above the corner grocery store. SROs were places nobody really knew existed, and yet were all around us. Simply put, single-room-occupancy is a generic term used to describe a living unit for (usually) one individual, that contains as little as 70 square feet, up to 200 square feet, with little or no cooking facilities, and a shared bath. That is about as close as you can get and take in just about every type of SRO that exists.

SROs have always been and continue to be the most affordable housing on the market. If you think of the housing market as a ladder, SROs are the bottom row of that ladder. The next step up would be a studio, above that would be an apartment and above that a single-family home and so on.

SROs take many different forms. Some could be referred to as boarding houses, where a person rents a room in a house and some type of food is provided. This is probably the earliest form of SRO that existed. It traditionally served mostly middle-class professional people, such as people employed as sales clerks. There are also residential hotels or what some people around the country call the "workingman's" hotel, which could have 100 to 300 units, with each unit having around 100 sq. ft. There are also rooming houses, cage hotels,[1] and first-class hotels that became residential hotels when the neighborhoods in which they were located fell on hard times. Then there are commercial traveler hotels, which can be anywhere from 60 to 90 units of 50 to 180 sq. ft., that traditionally served people who were coming into the city on business, again more of a working-class/middle-class person. These examples illustrate the range of buildings that fall into the category of single-room occupancy housing.

A prominent facet of SROs is that they have a front desk. It is usually operated 24 hours a day, 7 days a week. The front desk is where residents get their mail and their messages, and it is sort of "control central" for an SRO. The front desk controls who comes in, who goes out - the building rules are generally very strict about overnight guests. Most hotels don't allow overnight guests at all as a way to prevent people from doubling and tripling up in a unit. And there are other rules that are different than you would ever find in a multi-family building.

SROs tend to be places where even though people are single, they socialize quite a bit. People help each other, they do favors for each other, so that living in an SRO becomes a very important facet of a person's social life. A lot of elderly people live in SROs, people on fixed incomes who worked their whole lives and cannot afford to live anywhere else.

SROs often provide many different services to residents. They can even act as unofficial social workers. In fact, a lot of SRO operators know more than a lot of social workers.

History of SRO Housing

SROs were built by the hundreds of thousands around the country in the early part of this century. While there was a nonprofit market, most were built by private developers to meet the demand for low-cost housing in urban areas where the transient working population had grown tremendously. The need for transient workers came as a result of the industrial boom between 1870 and 1920, when workers were needed to build the new railroads and the infrastructures of urban areas.

SROs were designed to "maximize density and provide for the minimal needs of urban migrants," who were poor, transient working people. In Chicago, four lodging areas, or "stems", eventually formed off of the downtown area. These four stems were located along South State Street; outdoors in Grant Park near the Illinois Central tracks and the Art Institute; north Clark Street and Bughouse Square; and the most important stem of all, called the "Main" stem, which was on West Madison Street between Halsted and the Chicago River.

What has happened to SRO housing in the past seventy years since this form of housing appeared on the market? There has been a shift in the use of SROs from temporary shelter for transient workers into longer term housing for the stable working poor class. There has also been, however, a shift in the attitude of public officials and the business community from supporting SRO housing to becoming proponents of its mass destruction. During the Urban Renewal rage of the 1960s, and since then during the development boom of the 1980s, the City of Chicago has destroyed over 70% of its original SRO stock, once estimated to be 35,000 units. Today advocates estimate there are at most 15,000 units remaining. Particularly critical is the fact that the city continues to lose approximately 550 units of SRO housing each year. At this rate, Chicago could lose most of the remaining stock by the year 2000. Nationally, homeless advocates put the loss of SROs at about two million units; only about one million units remain. It should be noted that some cities have lost their entire stock of SRO housing.

The impact of this loss of SRO units is connected to its contemporary use as permanent housing for very low-income single adults. In the late 1970s, homeless advocates across the country began to connect the rise in the homeless population with the destruction of SRO housing. As the number of SRO units decreased, the market shrank. Without an affordable alternative, literally tens of thousands of people were forced to turn to the streets or emergency shelters for housing assistance.

Dozens of nonprofit organizations were formed across the country to try to preserve the dwindling supply of SRO housing, and to re-house former SRO residents who had become part of the homeless ranks. But nonprofit advocates approached the SRO business differently than the private market. Nonprofits believed that there had to be on-site social services in SROs in order to help formerly homeless residents stabilize their lives. A well-run, affordable unit was only 50% of the housing solution; social services were the critical other half.

The success of groups like the Central City Concern in Portland, Oregon and the SRO Corporation in Los Angeles led to a new nonprofit industry addressing what has come to be known as "special needs housing". Special needs housing is devoted to housing and serving groups of people including the working poor, chronically mentally ill, recovering and active substance-abusers, and the homeless. These are all contemporary users of SRO housing.

The Creation of LakeFront SRO Corporation

In 1985, spurred by a study done by the Jewish Council on Urban Affairs and the Community Emergency Shelter Organization that documented the 70% loss of SRO housing in Chicago, a group of Uptown activists working in the homeless and shelter movements decided to create a nonprofit corporation that would work to preserve single-room occupancy housing exclusively and to provide housing for homeless people. They came together to create Lakefront SRO Corporation, the city's first nonprofit developer of exclusively SRO housing.

Headquartered in Uptown and Edgewater, Lakefront's mission was threefold: 1) to preserve the existing stock of 2,400 SRO units along the north lakefront; 2) to create permanent housing for those who were currently homeless in Uptown and Edgewater; and 3) to advocate public policies which would slow the loss of Chicago's SRO stock.

Since 1985, Lakefront has gone on to purchase and develop six SROs: the Harold Washington Apartments, a 70-unit SRO; the Malden Arms, an 86-unit building; the Miriam Apartments, a 66-unit SRO exclusively for women; the Carlton Terrace Apartments, 70 units; the Delmar Apartments, 163 units; and the Major Jenkins Apartments, 163 units. In all we have developed 615 units of housing in six sites.

Financing and Acquisition of SROs

Lakefront has learned that "who you serve" is the primary issue to be determined before even thinking about developing a building. We had decided that our target population was low-income single adults whose incomes were between $2,000 and $5,000 per year. This dictated all our financing and acquisition decisions. The goal for the range of rents then had to be at least $50/month, and up to no more than $270/month. Knowing that, it became the objective of the real estate development team to make sure that debt service and operating expenses were kept in line with what our target homeless population could afford to pay. This meant, of course, that we could not obtain a conventional mortgage from the private market, and therefore had to obtain all our financing through government-related programs.

A typical "deal" for us includes:

- the City of Chicago: CDBG or HOME funds,

- the Illinois Housing Development Authority and the Illinois Affordable Housing Trust Fund,

- low-income housing tax credit syndication proceeds,

- and the Department of Housing and Urban Development SRO Sec. 8 Program or the City of Chicago Low-Income Housing Trust Fund for rent subsidy funds.

We believe in a gut rehab in order to keep operating costs down. Since it is unlikely we will be able to refinance our buildings after fifteen years, we want to get most of the work done upfront and not have the specter of, for example, a defunct heating system facing us in ten years. The more we do upfront, the lower our operating costs are, and the more secure our operating figures are for the future.[2]

FIGURE 2

What Does it Cost to Create
Affordable SRO Housing?

Project: 86 unit SRO with private baths, substantial rehab, individual kitchens, located in the Sheridan Park Historic District in Uptown.

Expenses	Subsidized Loan		Bank Loan	
Amount Borrowed:				
- City of Chicago	$	740,000		
- IAHTF		690,000	$	1,430,000
Term:	40 years		25 years	
Interest:	negotiated payment		9.5%	
Annual Payment	$	29,600	$	150,000
Mortgage Cost/Unit/month	$	29	$	145
*Operating Exps/Unit	$	220	$	220
TOTAL MONTHLY RENT:	$	249	$	365.00

The Argument for Rent Subsidy
What Does it Cost to House a Homeless Person?

Government Subsidized rent:	$	249.00
Tenant Contrib. on T.A.:	-	50.00
Annual Income: $ 1,848.		
Rent not covered by tenant:		199.00

Government Subsidized rent:	$	249.00
Tenant Contrib. on SSI:	-	132.00
Annual Income: $ 4,800		
Rent not covered by tenant:	$	117.00

* This total does not include the cost of social services or profit to the owners.

Blended Management

This is the area that most distinguishes nonprofit SROs from private market methods. Both Property Management and Social Service programs operate on-site in each of our buildings, and each has its own distinct duties and responsibilities. At the same time, we see the programs as interrelated and we've developed an operational system that reflects this belief. We call it "Blended Management." Under blended management, staff members from property management and social service programs work closely together in organizational planning and day-to-day operations. Blended management is a philosophy that guides all decision-making regarding site selection, tenant selection, design and renovation, tenant programs, and resolving tenant problems. By blending the two program areas together, we've found that we can enhance our ability to anticipate and meet the needs of our tenants while operating our buildings efficiently. For example, both property management and social service staff work together to screen and select new tenants. Similarly, if a tenant is late paying rent, the property manager will inform the social service staff of the problem, who will then try to work out a solution with the tenant. As a result, an eviction may be avoided. The building's vacancy rate stays low, the retention rate stays high - and the tenant stays off the streets. We estimate that since May 1989, when we opened our first building, our retention rate has been 83 percent, which means that of all the people who move in, almost 90 percent stay, and that is our ultimate goal. They stay because of the services and the affordable unit we can provide.

Social Service Responsibilities

Lakefront's Social Service Program operates on site at each building. The program has three goals:

1. To help tenants maintain permanent housing: through case management, social workers help tenants identify and change behavior patterns which threaten their ability to stay in housing.

2. To enhance individual well-being and build a sense of community in each building: to address the crippling sense of isolation and lack of self-esteem that homelessness causes, we provide social activities which build community.

3. To empower residents to take active roles in their buildings and the larger community: we do this through tenant advisory councils which are formed in each building. Tenants get together to work on management issues, social service issues, and larger community issues.

We average one social worker for every thirty tenants in each building.

We are also in the process of further clarifying who we serve through a system of separating clients into three categories:

Level 1: the most dependent population; usually chronic alcoholics and substance abusers; dually-diagnosed people;

Level 2: more independent than Level 1, have some ability to cope independently;

Level 3: the most independent population that we serve.

Exactly who is placed in each type of level is not determined by their problem so much as by their ability to cope with the "normal" day-to-day world. This can mean that a Level 3 building has active alcoholics in it who are coping better with the problem than others might who live in a Level 1 building.

We have found that the design and layout of buildings can vary significantly depending on the designated population in a building. By altering the design and building rules, we can more effectively serve those who are some of the most difficult-to-house of the homeless, and who we were not previously able to serve when we were only providing a certain style of housing, as in our Harold Washington Apartments. We wanted to be able to reach deeper into the homeless population.[4]

Property Management Responsibilities

The goals of the Property Management Program are twofold:

1. ensure the economic viability of each building: lease the units, pay the bills, collect the rent; and

2. maintain a safe, secure, and decent environment for the residents: fix the plumbing, keep the building clean, staff the sites, provide all the basic amenities that any tenant would expect.

Staffing for Property Management includes 24-hour desk coverage at each building, seven-day-a-week janitorial services, part-time maintenance services, a site manager for each building, and a Director of Property Management who supervises all of the property staff. Property management is very labor intensive for both nonprofit organizations and the private market. It is also very expensive to manage an SRO. The front desk alone costs $45,000 a year (we pay more than most equivalent operators do: benefits and a minimum-wage salary). It is a lot of money to have to spread across the units, but it is needed in order to control what is going on in the buildings.

Community Relations

The Uptown and Edgewater communities have a history of conflict over the development of low-income housing, and this is particularly true of SRO housing. People say that the buildings are full of prostitutes and drug addicts. In some cases that is true, although often an SRO will blend into the community so well that people won't even know it exists until it develops a problem—and then the community wants it shut down.

In 1986 when Lakefront was first being formed, the Board took the position that we had to openly and respectfully come to the community with our mission. We took the road that the community had specific and legitimate issues of concern about the management, tenant selection, and rehab of the buildings. We decided to go to people early with what we were doing. That, as a strategy, has served us extremely well.

One of my first tasks when I was hired in 1987 was to do community outreach to all sectors of the neighborhood—religious, business, and civic—to inform the community about what we wanted to do. Later on a program was created that is devoted exclusively to community education about SRO housing. Since 1987, we have organized hundreds of tours of our buildings, reaching thousands of people. We actively participate in community institutions, and we work the P.R. angle quite a bit. The result of all our community outreach and involvement is that we have an excellent relationship with the neighborhood and have had not one community group or block club oppose our development of any site. This is not to say that we do not have our detractors; there are some who would prefer that the SROs be torn down to having a nonprofit developer come in. However, we have created a middle ground where we can reach an accommodation with most people.

By having high quality property management services and on-site social service programs, we handle 90% of the concerns of most residents in the neighborhood. Also, our excellent rehab work brings up the value of local real estate, which does not go unnoticed by local residents.

Will this situation continue indefinitely? Will the neighborhood allow us to keep purchasing buildings endlessly? Probably not. In addition, our ability to develop exclusively in Uptown is also hampered by the City's desire to spread its SRO development dollars to neighborhoods on the south and west sides as well. Inevitably, then, we will develop SRO housing in areas other than Uptown/Edgewater.

I cannot underestimate the importance of developing relationships with significant community leaders and city leaders who can build bridges for an organization like ours. Private SRO operators have also come to benefit from the work that nonprofits and others have done in building bridges between lenders and SRO operators, who before were seen as a sector of the housing market that no one wanted to serve. These types of institutional leaders can have a great effect on creating support for a neighborhood group like ours, and the reality is that friends are important in the development business.

Conclusion

The history of SRO housing reveals that there have always been alternatives to the traditional single family home in this country. From the rooming houses and workingman's hotels of the past, to the nonprofit model of SRO housing as we know it today, a market for this type of "shared housing" has always existed, and there have always been landlords to supply it, both for-profit and nonprofit.

The SRO has evolved through the years: from housing transient workers, to providing permanent living space for the "working poor" and retired people, to today's multi-faceted role of housing the working poor, retired people, people who were previously homeless, people who are chronically mentally ill, and substance abusers. The original shared housing characteristics of SRO-type housing—the 24-hour desk clerks, the common areas, shared bathrooms and kitchens, the sense of community that often emerged—have been broadened and developed by nonprofit developers to meet the needs of the new SRO population. In that sense, what we are doing is nothing new, we are building on a tradition.

But what is new is the growing recognition of the importance and validity of this type of housing. There has always been more to America than the suburban single-family home, and finally we are starting to see public acceptance of this fact. Hopefully this growing acceptance will lead to support—if not the same level of support that single family housing receives through the massive subsidy program known as the home mortgage interest deduction, then at least government and private sector encouragement in the form of low cost financing and subsidy programs that enable SROs to serve people at the lowest end of the economic scale. Without this support, the economics of today's housing market will cause this valuable housing resource to finally disappear.

The longterm prognosis for SROs still looks bleak, despite the positive current activity. Though new programs are being created, we are still losing many more units than are being saved and added to the market today. And the homeless population is growing—that trend doesn't appear to be letting up.

But nonprofits like ours can make the point that there are positive solutions to the homeless problem and to providing housing for single, low-income people. With the success of models like Lakefront, we can continue to make that argument to people in the government and private sector who are in a position to do something about the problem. As long as there is a problem, groups like ours need to exist and to do this kind of work.

Notes

1. Very few cage hotels are left. They consist of a large room that was chopped-up into cubicles of 60 or 70 square feet. To get around the housing code, which required a window per unit, the cubicles were separated by walls that did not go quite to the ceiling to allow for ventilation. But because the walls do not go from floor to ceiling between each unit, they put matting or chicken wire across the top of the wall to prevent people from crawling into each other's cubicle. That is how they get the name "chicken coop" or "cage" hotels. I found it impossible to photograph a cubicle because they were so small—all that is inside is a bed against the wall, usually a dresser, and a few hooks to hang up some things. The Wilson Men's Club is a cage hotel of 260 units and it costs $260 a month to live there, or $7.50 a night. Though it sounds horrible, it is home for a lot of people who can't afford anything else. Actually it is run fairly well, and is always full except in the summertime which people will sleep outside in the parks to save a little month.

2. We spend about $25,00 per unit in rehab along. It is expensive: when we rehabbed the Malden Arms, for example, we needed to maintain the standards of the state Historic Preservation Authority. When we're all done, after we bought a buidling and renovated it, after all of our soft costs and attorneys' fees, it costs us between $32,000 and $40,000 per unit. We

believe that it is a good investment because we intend to own these buildings for the next 30 years and we want a quality product.

3. We got involved in working on a Level 1 building, the Del Mar Apartments (164 units), because the alderman came to us and said "Look, this is the worst building in my ward and no one wants to do anything with it, short of shutting it down. Can you do something with it?" After we had seen it, we realized that is was going to be really tough, but we recognized that the residents were already dealing with a difficult situation, and that this is what people do. We don't believe that we're creating something that doesn't already exist. We're going in and trying to manage something and make it better, not evict or displace people because we have middle-class standards.

4. The decision to expand the types of buildings we provide was based on our experience in interviewing potential tenants. We looked at who we were rejecting all the time, the people we thought couldn't make it into the Washington Apartments (Level 3). We began to understand the pattern of what was happening, and that the design of our buildings, to a large degree, was making it impossible for us to serve people who were really dependent and had serious problems. For example, Level 1 buildings need hotplates with timers and timed faucets, and some housekeeping services. Level 3 units have regular cooktops.

In the Miriam Apartments that are only for women, we installed community kitchens, one on each floor or one for each 12 women, because we think community kitchens will help create a sense of community for these women who are often very isolated and often experiencing a prolonged recovery from being victims of violence.

The other problem is that you can't mix the kinds of people who are in the Del Mar (Level 1) necessarily with people who are in the Washington, because in order to manage the Del Mar population you must have strict rules, such as restricting where visitors can go or whether and how often visitors can stay overnight, and the people who live in the Washington would never put up with it—they don't need that, so why should they? Social service programs also differ. Level 1 programs include basic living skills and food skills training, like how to clean, take a bath, or go shopping.

CHAPTER 7

Abbeyfield: Community-Based Shared Housing for the Elderly

Richard Biddlecombe

This chapter explains the origin and concepts of Abbeyfield, and the principles which have guided its rapid growth in the United Kingdom and more recently across the world. I hope to impart the reasons for the enthusiasm felt by Abbeyfield volunteers. Abbeyfield is a volunteer-led organization that helps provide shared housing for mainly single people over 65 in communities where they usually have existing social contacts. Each house is independent, with its own developers, managers, and residents, yet is connected to a national organization that provides recommendations for structure and management as well as fund-raising support. Houses are of two types. Supportive Care houses accommodate residents who are reasonably able-bodied. The term "Supportive Care" house is now steadily being replaced by the phrase "Very Sheltered" housing. Extra Care houses shelter residents who require personal and medical attention. A few are also registered as part nursing homes.

In the spectrum of housing to care, Abbeyfield falls between sheltered accommodation and full nursing facilities. We offer an excellent way of filling the all-important gap between complete independence and the need for full nursing. In the United Kingdom, sheltered housing is accommodation for married or single people, normally in a block of self-contained apartments. A Site Manager is usually available to deal with minor emergencies and to ensure that the correct services are contacted in the case of a major emergency, e.g., calling a doctor or ambulance. Some sheltered housing schemes in the United Kingdom have communal dining and living areas, with lunch provided, at extra cost. At the other end of the spectrum there is the nursing home. These establishments provide for personal and nursing care, usually falling short of hospitalization.

Abbeyfield sits between these two forms of caring. It would not suit those who happily prefer to live alone, who dislike sharing or not being the permanent focal point of a group, who need advanced nursing or have a severe mental disability. While the Abbeyfield concept of care is not the answer to everybody's prayers, Abbeyfield has been proven to be an excellent alternative to what else is available. Without Abbeyfield, people would:

> 1. Remain alone in their own home, which could lead to depression, a poor diet, and to a growing sense of insecurity. The UK Government's current thinking and the thinking of some other charities is that elderly people are better off in their own home with care taken to them. While that is admirable for those who truly wish to be alone, it does little to help those who don't. I am rather skeptical that this view is taken mainly for economic reasons rather than humanitarian beliefs.

> 2. Move in with relatives. In the long run, though, that is rarely the ideal situation and depending upon the accommodation available, the family relationship could deteriorate to the detriment of all concerned.

> 3. Move into sheltered accommodation. Yet again, for the person who is unwilling or unable to live alone, this solves nothing. The site manager is not available on a regular day-to-day basis to comfort residents who are lonely or unable to cope with their daily chores.

> 4. Finally, there is the local (Government, District, or State) home or the private nursing home. The former houses 40–50 residents and the latter from 10–50. Both operations are managed and run by paid administrators and staff, and usually cater for those who are very frail. They provide full personal and nursing care. Those elderly people with little money would normally end up in a local authority home while the more affluent are likely to move into a private commercial nursing home of their choice. While some homes are a good value with excellent care facilities, in others the commercial priorities tend to blur the reasons for the establishment's existence.

Introduction to Abbeyfield

The overview of the organization and its present structure are as follows:

Abbeyfield International

National Society

Local Society

Executive Committee

House Committee

Housekeeper   House Manager & Staff
(Supportive House)   (Extra Care House)
Residents

Abbeyfield International (AI), a registered charity, was established in 1988 in response to an ever increasing number of inquiries from around the world. It offers advice and guidance to form new National Abbeyfield Societies in new countries and acts as a clearing house of information for existing members. Being a small charity, AI tends to use the publications and visual aids of the UK National Society to promote Abbeyfield.

Each **National Society** becomes a member of AI. The Abbeyfield Society (UK), where it all started, is the largest with over 1,000 houses and thirty-nine years of 'grass roots' experience honing the best way to present Abbeyfield to the community. A National Society registers all Local Societies in its country, monitors standards,[1] and provides information on development, changing legislation, and other matters of interest by way of publications, circular letters, seminars and so forth. It is the guardian of the Abbeyfield name, and represents the Abbeyfield movement in national affairs.

Local Societies, while members of their National Society, are legally autonomous. They agree to abide by the Guiding Principles of Abbeyfield (see Appendix A). While the concept of care remains the same, the management tends to vary slightly from house to house. Local Societies are run by volunteers via two Committees. The Executive Committee considers policy and the House Committee oversees the day-to-day running of the house. It is essential that each house is financially self-sufficient.

The **Housekeeper in a Supportive Care house** (7–10 residents) and the **House Manager in an Extra Care house** (20–36 residents) are responsible for the actual running of the house. In Supportive houses the Housekeeper is the only full time member of staff. She/He provides the main meals of the day and generally acts as 'mother' to her 'family' of residents. In Extra Care, where the design of the house ensures that the 'family' principle is maintained, staff numbers are close to 1:1 as 24-hour personal care is offered, but rarely full nursing care, and all meals are provided.

Residents will be over retirement age (65 years) and generally reasonably able-bodied. Abbeyfield was formed to provide lonely older people with their own home within the security and companionship of a small family household. Most older people are too proud to admit to being lonely, and I prefer to substitute 'lonely older people' with the phrase 'those older people who are unable or unwilling to live alone.' Abbeyfield residents furnish their own bed-sitting room and are expected to be able to generally look after themselves and get to the dining room for meals. As they become frail, the Local Society will endeavor to increase staffing levels or buy in welfare services to ensure that they can remain in their Abbeyfield home. A few will eventually need regular personal care and it is likely they would then move into Extra Care. The residents are the most important part of Abbeyfield and we strive to improve their quality of life.

The Origins of the Abbeyfield Concept

The Abbeyfield concept is a simple one, thought of by a man of vision. Major Richard Carr-Gomm spent most of his childhood in Bermondsey, London, part of the Docklands area of the River Thames, where most of the residents were poor and under-privileged. Travelling the world as a Coldstream Guard, he was regularly reminded of Bermondsey and his childhood by the poverty he saw in the many countries he visited. Richard frequently returned to Bermondsey, which had been badly damaged in the German raids, and witnessed the loneliness, insecurity and the despair of many older people. Their retirement pension was sufficient to manage on and the rent of a single room was not exorbitant, but often the landlords cheated or ill-treated their aging residents.

Richard resigned his commission in 1955 to dedicate his life to caring for older people. Moving back to Bermondsey, he found work as a Home Help—assisting those who were in some way unable fully to fend for themselves, and had nobody else to help them. The lonely shallow lives of his clients had a profound effect on him. After he called upon an old man and found that he had been lying flat on his face on the floor for almost 24 hours without anyone to help him, he resolved to find a new home for some of these people, where they could be cared for and secure while regaining their dignity and independence. He was able to buy a small, condemned house with six small rooms, a tiny kitchen, and an outside toilet. He furnished and decorated it with the help of his friends in a Christian group, and it opened for its first residents on December 17th 1955.

The first two residents were a lady of 81 years and a gentleman of 79. Richard acted as the housekeeper, or mother to the family, and within a week or two, word got out that it was wonderful to have everything clean and tidy, meals provided, and people calling to see them. He involved the families of the residents and neighbors in supporting the residents in the house. It was soon clear that a permanent housekeeper would be necessary for Richard's cooking skills were limited! The residents paid a modest charge, probably equating to the rent paid for their former properties and the housekeeper, who was provided with modest accommodation, received a small wage. The project was viable. Richard had provided two lonely older people with their own home within the security and companionship of a small family-style household. They had regained their dignity while retaining a strong sense of privacy and independence. Richard was suddenly inundated with requests for the two remaining slots. He and his team mounted fund-raising campaigns. Within a year, there were five houses. The idea rapidly caught on, and it was agreed a legal entity had to be set up to monitor the schemes, both present and future. A National Society was established to register 'Local Societies', monitor standards, maintain a database of experiences, and give advice and guidance to newcomers. The Company was registered as a charity. A simple statement of beliefs, known as the Guiding Principles of Abbeyfield, was drawn up. They remain the cornerstone of the movement today (Appendix A).

The Structure of Abbeyfield

Abbeyfield is led by volunteers. Without volunteers, Abbeyfield would not exist today. Each Abbeyfield house project starts with, initially, one volunteer in an area learning of the Abbeyfield concept of care, believing it would fill a need in that person's local community, and building a resolve to strive to fill that need. That volunteer of vision would then persuade friends and associates to join a small team to undertake a feasibility study leading, hopefully, to a successful project.

On the basis of an affirmative feasibility study, a Local Abbeyfield Society is formed, with the agreement of and affiliated to the National Abbeyfield Society. That is necessary to ensure all societies wishing to use the name Abbeyfield maintain high standards of which the organization can be justly proud. The local society becomes incorporated and also registers as a charity. Its affiliation to the National Society does not affect its operation as an autonomous body. It receives guidance from the center but does not have to listen, providing it keeps within the broad Guiding Principles of Abbeyfield. Informational manuals provide recommendations on structure and organization of houses.

All Committees in local Societies, i.e., Executive and House Committees, consist entirely of volunteers. They manage the Society, ensuring that the houses operate efficiently and in a happy atmosphere. The Society has overall responsibility for the well-being of the residents and for maintaining the property in good order. Volunteers, by regular visiting, gain the confidence of residents and learn of problems and also ideas for the house. Additionally, the residents' representative on the House Committee (and sometimes Executive Committee) can speak for all residents at committee meetings. As with a normal family, it is not difficult to sense when there is a problem. Volunteer numbers vary with each Society. Much will depend on the time individuals can devote to the Society. The minimum is probably six where individuals undertake more than one task. The ideal is nearer twelve, including such professionals as an accountant, attorney, doctor, social worker, architect, nurse, secretary, and care-givers. Every Society is encouraged to have an Honorary Medical Advisory on its Executive Committee. This is to ensure that prospective residents are suitable for the care a local Society can offer. They have a medical examination as part of their application to join a house, and the doctor's recommendation is accepted. The volunteers, through the Executive and House Committees, will decide policy and financial matters, and support the housekeeper and residents through regular visiting.

Only the housekeeper (in Canada—house parent) in each house is a full-time, paid employee. This is a fundamental difference between Abbeyfield and most other housing groups. She has the protection of government employment legislation. She has set hours of work but is expected to be flexible. A relief housekeeper is employed to cover absences. Ideally they work a five-day week, with two days off during the week that can be taken as a weekend once a month. They have a minimum of twenty vacation days per year. The Society provides a self-contained flat, preferably with two bedrooms, a lounge/diner, kitchen, and bathroom. In older properties one bedroom is more normal. Each house provides a guest room which is used by the relief housekeeper during the housekeeper's absence. Occasionally volunteers provide the meals for the residents and sleep in during the housekeeper's absence, thereby helping to reduce the costs of the Society. As each Society is autonomous, the running of each house will differ slightly as will the arrangements to cover the housekeeper's absences.

The housekeeper cooks the two main meals of the day, for which all residents come together, and is on call at night should a resident have a problem. While the housekeeper is required to sleep in when on duty, she is not tied to the house 24 hours a day. After providing the main meals of the day and undertaking her other duties of managing the day-to-day running of the house, she is free to come and go as she pleases. Other paid support staff include a part-time cook, housecleaner, and gardener.

The first Abbeyfield house became known as a 'Supportive' care house and the vast majority of houses today are of this type, accommodating able-bodied older people. For economic reasons the recommended number of residents has increased from 4–5 in the early houses to 7–10 today. Each resident's bed-sitting room has a wash basin or en-suite facilities wherever possible (especially in new buildings), and an electric point specifically for an electric kettle to make a hot drink whenever they wish.

To help residents as they become frail, Societies add extra fitments to a house to help the residents' mobility and comfort, such as hand rails, an elevator, special handles on taps, and special baths with hydraulic seats. Should temporary personal care be required by a resident it can be bought in at extra cost. Staffing may also be increased to 24-hour cover with all meals provided and a laundry and room cleaning service. This is called "Extended Care". The enhanced facilities enable Societies to register with Social Services to offer personal care if they so wish. To cover the extra costs properties might be extended to, say, sixteen residents, providing much additional welcome revenue.

Abbeyfield promotes a 'one move' policy for its residents, but that is not always possible, so we also have Extra Care houses for very frail residents. These accommodate up to 36 residents and provide full personal care, and very occasionally full nursing. Staffing levels are naturally much higher than in a Supportive house and the charges reflect that position.

Prospective residents usually hear about Abbeyfield through word of mouth via friends, older persons' clubs, churches, or by reading notices in doctors' offices or at the local library. Societies ensure they are well-known to local doctors and Social Services Departments and thereby receive referrals from those sources. In the UK the average age of residents in Supportive houses twenty years ago was the early 70s. Now it is nearer the early 80s with residents even coming in at over 90! In Extra Care the average age is late 80s.[2]

The emphasis on lonely people, or those unable or unwilling to live alone, stresses the point that Abbeyfield was formed for single people. A few houses have used large rooms to take in couples, but that has usually not proved very effective. Couples tended to keep together, quite naturally, not allowing themselves to become truly part of the 'family' within the Abbeyfield house. We lay great store by the fact that Abbeyfield gives back the 'family', and through that real 'companionship', to its residents while enabling them to retain their dignity and independence. Abbeyfield gives the resident the chance to participate fully in a close 'family' environment, sharing meals together, happy events, and also sadnesses. The housekeeper cultivates the bond of friendship in the group that ensures a happy family unit.

A typical prospective resident would be a single person, living alone in the local community or who has connections, such as relatives, with that community. That person would be finding it difficult to cope on their own, perhaps through the loss of a loved one, or with the cooking, or the usual problems of running one's own home. As they grow older they may well experience fears about their safety; fear of burglary or even mugging. Their link with the local community helps them to feel at ease and usually ensures that there will always be someone other than Committee Members and volunteers to visit them. If they are happy in the community besides being happy in their Abbeyfield family, they are more likely to participate in community activities which are encouraged by each Society, e.g. Seniors Clubs, Bowls Clubs, Film Clubs etc. Many Societies also provide some regular activities for their residents.

I am, in a volunteer capacity, Chairman of the local Abbeyfield Society in Potters Bar in England where we have two Supportive houses. I will describe how three typical residents came to us. The first was a lady who came from a rundown part of North London where she felt it had become dangerous to go out at any time of the day for fear of having her handbag snatched or her flat burgled. The other two residents had both lost their wives. The first had the opportunity to live with one of his several children but chose Abbeyfield so that he could retain his independence from his blood relatives while not losing the companionship of a 'family'. He was able to remain near his own family but not impinge on their freedom, and retain his independence. The other gentleman had retired and moved from the town where he grew up and worked to a rural area nearby. He was recently widowed, his health deteriorated, and he became introverted. His friends told me recently that the move to Abbeyfield, gave him a new lease on life. At 83 years of age, he remains an active Rotarian, a good friend of Abbeyfield and father figure to the other residents.

Residents usually come into Abbeyfield through Supportive houses. Some have disabilities. Some are partially sighted, others have mild arthritis, a heart condition, diabetes, or other reasonably well-controlled medical conditions. With only a housekeeper looking after the residents in the Supportive house, we cannot take in very frail people. As their health deteriorates, residents' care can be increased, regrettably at a price. Ultimately they might need to move to an Extra Care house and in exceptional cases into a non-Abbeyfield nursing home or hospital.

Charges for living in an Abbeyfield house are kept to a minimum because of the high level of volunteer support. Residents' charges usually average $112–176 per week, although newly built projects can work out to

$240 per week. The charge includes the provision of central heating, lighting, use of laundry facilities, and the provision of meals. The resident's only additional expense, other than personal items, is usually the cost of a private telephone. A public telephone is provided in each house.

In the United Kingdom, and in other countries too, there are several levels of government financial support available to the older person, whether they are in an Abbeyfield house or trying to exist on their own. While approximately half of Abbeyfield residents in the United Kingdom pay their own way without help from the government, Abbeyfield is designed to be affordable by everyone, regardless of ability to pay. All United Kingdom citizens over 65 years receive a state retirement pension, which is currently $87 per week, for a single person. The local societies who run the houses are not interested in the financial affairs of the individual, only that the weekly charge will be met. It is inevitable, however, that in the family grouping that is established, the Chairman of the House Committee invariably learns about most residents' financial situation, for those who need to apply for the various benefits frequently get confused in filling out the claim forms and seek assistance.

The principal benefits for senior citizens in the United Kingdom include Income Support, administered by the Department of Social Security (DSS). Of the two levels of payment, the top rate of $328 per week, plus a personal allowance of $20, can usually only be claimed by residents in Extra Care. For those in Supportive care, the payment is a maximum of $280 per week, plus the $20 personal allowance. It is not a straight hand-out. The DSS will cover the difference between a person's income, including state pension, and the Abbeyfield weekly charge. The personal allowance is paid in addition. The first $4,800 of assets owned by a resident is disregarded. For every $400 over the first $4,800, up to a figure of $12,800, it is assumed that the resident could receive interest of $1.60 per week. Therefore with $6,800 savings, the first $4,800 would be ignored but the DSS would assume that the resident receives $8 per week on the remaining $2,000. That sum would be added to the resident's actual income before the level of income support was calculated.

Another benefit, Housing Benefit, is administered by the Housing Department of the local government. It is intended to cover the cost of the provision of adequate accommodation including compulsory service charges such as cleaning, heating and lighting shared areas, gardening, window cleaning, etc. Because our residents are classed as a vulnerable group, the local government has very limited powers to restrict the amounts paid as Housing Benefit. The complicated calculation involves both a breakdown of a resident's charge and an individual's income. Not all the items covered by Abbeyfield's charge can be taken into account, e.g., food, fuel costs for residents, and water rates. As with Income Support, savings of less than $4,800 are disregarded, but the upper qualifying limit is $25,600, so that anyone with more than this would not be eligible for the housing benefit. Those with savings between $4,802 and $25,600 are assumed to receive an income of $1.60 per week for each $400 of capital in the same way that the DSS operates.

Some residents will qualify for an Attendance Allowance which, unlike the other benefits, is not means tested but dependent upon medical eligibility. From April 1993, the lower rate, either a day rate or a night rate, was fixed at $46.32 per week with the higher rate covering 24-hour attendance at $70.32 per week. The benefit is also administered by the Department of Social Security.

For Supportive houses, the charges are always below the lower Income Support level and therefore Abbeyfield is truly affordable by all. In Extra Care, where personal care is given, staff costs are higher and therefore the weekly charge is considerably more and frequently slightly above the maximum level of Income Support. However, it is the Society's firm intention not to ask residents to leave because their personal funds have been exhausted or because a gap has appeared between the benefit receivable and the weekly charge. Societies are working hard to build up endowment funds to cover such situations, and there are charitable trusts and foundations who will provide help to individual residents.

The Abbeyfield idea grew rapidly and has been exported around the world, frequently by Abbeyfielders emigrating. Today there are some 700 local Societies, managing 1,100 Supportive houses, with the help of 15,000 volunteers, accommodating 9,000 residents, in ten countries—Australia, Canada, Ireland, Italy, Jersey, Netherlands, New Zealand, Scotland, South Africa, and the United Kingdom. It is particularly interesting to note that in Australia, it took six years to achieve the first house in 1986. Today there are ten, and all the houses accommodate people on very low incomes. As in Canada, it is expected that in the future the number of houses open will increase by two to three houses per year. The Abbeyfield Society of the USA is currently being formed and the first Abbeyfield opened in Brookfield, Illinois, through the good offices of The British Home, on March 25, 1995. There are also interested parties in such diverse countries as Argentina, Belgium, Chile, Cyprus, France, Jamaica, Japan, Poland, and Spain.

The majority of houses are currently in the UK, including 45 Extra Care houses. With so many houses in the UK, one can usually find at least one house in most towns of any size, and several in each city. For example, Edinburgh has 30 houses including four Extra Care houses and Belfast has 25, all Supportive houses. The Abbeyfield concept of care remains broadly the same in each country but it is interesting to see how local customs, culture, and resources affect the houses. In the vast countries of Australia and Canada, for example, houses tend to be bungalow style (one floor only), many built in wood. In the UK, most are two story and brick conversions. The position is similar in Ireland and South Africa. In the Netherlands one house occupies the self-contained ground floor of an apartment block, with secure entrances. It is our experience that older people tend to want to live with their own nationals, to share their culture and religion. While every house is open to all older people, it is not surprising that Societies have started and are operated by and for different ethnic groups. For instance there are Afro-Caribbean, Chinese, Jewish, Polish, Sachkhand Nanak Dam (Indian), and Vietnamese Societies. The houses operate on similar lines to every other house although menus can be somewhat different![3]

How a Local Society Establishes an Abbeyfield House

As previously mentioned, each Abbeyfield house begins with an interested individual who pulls together a team of friends and associates to form a local Society. The path of a Society intent on providing an Abbeyfield house in their community is broadly as follows. The volunteer team that has been drawn together becomes a working committee, elects a chairman, and seeks registration as a new Society with the National Society. It also registers as a separate charity. The local Society then considers what it would like to do and how it might be done, having regard to recommended design standards, etc. The National Society offers guidance, which is invariably sought. The first task of the committee is to confirm that a need exists in the community for an Abbeyfield house. Discussions take place with the Area Health Authority, Area Social Services and the local district governmental authority. In the United Kingdom, these bodies are aware of the work Abbeyfield undertakes. It is very important that the local Society build and maintain a good rapport with the local authorities, i.e., the providers of services, funding, planning authorizations, etc.

If all agree that a project is needed, the committee considers how that elusive first house might be obtained. Should they purchase or lease an existing property and convert it, or might they be fortunate enough to find a vacant piece of land for a new building? It is likely they would purchase, extend, and convert, for few existing house can accommodate sufficient residents, or have the necessary facilities readily available. However, there are several examples of other procedures.

Volunteers know their community and what is available, and they can assess the cost implications. They consider how the project could be funded. In the UK, The Housing Corporation, effectively a funding arm of the Government set up to fund house building, will support projects in inner city areas and for minority ethnic groups. Commercial mortgages at beneficial rates can be obtained and with fund-raising appeals to companies, trusts, foundations, and by a series of varied fund-raising events, the committed Society succeeds! Our Societies' fund-raising efforts frequently involve Rotary, Round Table, Lions, Soroptimists and many other such community service clubs, all good friends of Abbeyfield, both in the UK and across the world. Occasionally joint ventures with other organizations take place, perhaps with a church group or a welfare association. Even so, establishing a house can take several years from inception to completion and there will be many frustrations along the way.

A Supportive House: The Abbeyfield Liss Society

A typical example of a Supportive house scheme involved a group of volunteers in Liss, a small town in Hampshire, who formed the Abbeyfield Liss Society in 1965. The rector of the local church was told by one of his parishioners that he was having considerable problems with his sister-in-law. She was a widow who was very unhappy living alone. The rector knew of a number of other lonely elderly people. Having heard of Abbeyfield, the rector and the parishioner agreed to pursue the matter and gathered together more parishioners into a volunteer group. They found a lovely, large house with extensive grounds close to the church. The parishioner agreed to buy the house for $21,000 initially and, once the Abbeyfield Liss Society was formed, a mortgage was obtained and the parishioner was repaid. Only modest alterations were undertaken and the house was soon open. The layout was not ideal but adequate to get started. There were six resident's rooms but minimal accommodation for the housekeeper, with a bedroom upstairs and a living room downstairs, and shared bathroom facilities with the residents.

Selecting the residents to be the first family proved quite difficult despite all of the residents coming from the locality. In addition, the committee learned that they were not experienced in choosing a housekeeper and there were two bad appointments before the ideal one was made. That housekeeper stayed with the Society for fourteen years, looking after not only the residents, but an invalid husband. While the initial year or so proved problematic, the house became a real 'family' home and has remained so to this day.

In the mid-1980s a revitalized committee recognized that the accommodation was inadequate for the residents and particularly for the housekeeper. Also the small number of residents was beginning to affect the financial viability of the house. When the committee voted to upgrade the house, dissenting committee members resigned and further volunteers were sought. The National Society was asked to send a representative to discuss plans to alter and extend the house to accommodate nine residents in all, provide self-contained accommodation for the housekeeper, a guest room for the relief housekeeper, and an office, and to comply with the current fire regulations. An architect was employed to draw up plans for the alterations, the cost of which increased from $192,000 to $320,000. A mortgage of $160,000, at preferential rates, was taken from a building society and a $32,000 interest-free loan was given by the Abbeyfield National Society. Once the decision was made to go ahead, the local Society raised $128,000.

When the work began in 1988, it was necessary to empty the house of residents. One went to stay in the guest room of the local Extra Care house, another moved to a nearby Abbeyfield house and the remaining four went to stay with friends and relatives. On completion of the renovation, an Open Day was held to thank all the people who had contributed their efforts. As the visitors toured the public rooms, they found them furnished with carpets, tables, chairs, pictures, and crockery was laid out in the kitchen. Each item was priced. The visitors were asked yet again to put their hand in their pocket to buy an article for the house. The occasion was a great success for we all prefer to see what we are actually purchasing when we support a charity. The local Society regularly holds fund-raising events for further improvements to the house and also to provide an endowment fund for residents who move to Extra Care and find there is a gap between the charges and their income, whether it is bolstered by Income Support or not. (Weekly charges at this house vary between $172 and $260, depending on the size of the room.)

The housekeeper retired when renovations began, and a new one was appointed some six weeks before the house re-opened so that she could get used to the house, come to know the committee, and see the residents return to the house over a period of weeks. Once again, several residents had to be found to fill the new rooms. An Applications and Admissions Secretary was appointed to keep in touch with and assess prospective residents with the House Chairman. Occasionally there is an 'unsuitable resident'—perhaps one who has been unable to settle, despite a trial period as a prospective resident, or one who later becomes disruptive. Naturally they would be counselled over a period of time, by the House Chairman, and eventually with medical support. If that proved unsuccessful then they would be asked to find alternative accommodation. In the interests of that resident, the other residents, and the housekeeper, we would ultimately take legal action to move the person on if that became necessary. Fortunately that is seldom the case, but it has happened.

The Liss Society has two examples which illustrate the success of Abbeyfield's concept of care. One resident, who is now ninety and has been at the house for two years, lived on a street where everybody went out to work. She rarely saw anybody during the day and in the evening her neighbors had their own families to care for. She decided to come into Abbeyfield against her son's will, for he thought it was just another institution. Her son now admits that it was the best thing she could have done, for she is a changed person and has regained an interest in life. The second resident was in her early 80s. (I should stress that while most of the residents are ladies, there are many men in Abbeyfield houses.) She was living in a nursing home that cost $560 per week, sitting in a chair in the living room from morning until night vaguely staring at the walls and the ceiling. Her son was appalled, and in seeking alternative accommodation for her, he was directed to Abbeyfield. Not only were the charges less than a third of what he had been paying, the transformation of his mother was almost beyond belief. She is now, on a voluntary basis, a part-time teacher at the local junior school, helping the children learn to read.

An Extra Care House: The Abbeyfield Cambridge Society

The Abbeyfield Cambridge local Society was one of the first fifty Societies in the United Kingdom. It opened its first house in 1963 and added a house each year for the next six years, after which, for about ten years, it extended, replaced, and added to some houses. The total number of residents is now fifty with an average age of 85 years—a far cry from the first five residents whose ages were between 65–70 years of age. The lengthening lifespan became a challenge as early as 1970, when the Cambridge Society experienced the sadness of having to tell residents that they had become too heavy a responsibility for one housekeeper. The residents and their relatives understood in advance that they would have to make other arrangements. The Society's only remaining obligations were patience and whatever helpful advice they could supply. Other Societies across the country were naturally experiencing the same phenomena and some were busy setting up other houses or wings with which to give that "Extra Care". This extension of care became the logical compliment to Supportive care. But Extra Care needed larger and more elaborately equipped houses and their capital funding posed formidable problems.

The Executive Committee of the Cambridge Society decided to accept the challenge and move into Extra Care. It was accepted that Extra Care would demand more complex and sustained application of time, skills, and zeal than are normally called for with Supportive care. However, this must not be misunderstood. Supportive care is the best training for Extra Care, because it serves as an inoculation against the menace of the "institutional" which inevitably looms over larger houses and more numerous staffs. The move from Supportive to Extra Care involves not changing the spirit that drives the machine, but shifting the same machine up to much higher gears.

After a couple of false starts, Cambridge accepted the advice of the National Society that Extra Care was not best undertaken by adding a wing to an existing Supportive house or by acquiring and converting an existing structure. Three senior members of the Executive Committee formed a Steering Committee and completed a feasibility study for a new building. An application was made for a Housing Association Grant. The Society was soon able to buy a half acre site within one and a half miles of the city center for $34,400 (it would cost $400,000 today). It was estimated the final cost would be $1.2 million. The proposed scheme won the Housing Corporation's approval in 1983 for a grant of $880,000, but budget constraints delayed their seeking bids for the construction work until the summer of 1984.

The Executive Committee, by then, had set up a Project Sub-Committee to get the project on-site and take it through to completion. This turned out to involve two years of hard labor. The Sub-Committee consisted of the Deputy Chairman and five members, each with one of the following functions: 1) chairmanship and contact with the architects; 2) contact with the funding body (The Housing Corporation) and their lawyers; 3) private fund-raising (for all needs not covered by HAG); 4) furnishings and garden design; 5) acquisition of equipment; 6) personnel—qualifications, numbers, and cost. Each member reported progress at monthly committee meetings, taking consensus guidance as necessary.

The Sub-Committee considered the draft architectural designs in detail, made their decisions, and then left it to the Chairman to follow through. "Second thoughts"—that dread of all architects—were thus almost completely avoided. The member handling private fund-raising chose a small working group of dynamic friends and handled the appeal from his personal office. About $208,000 was raised in two years, of which more than half came in two amounts; one from a local wealthy trust and the other from the executors of a lady's estate who had already favored the Society in her lifetime. For the rest, they "played the field" and in so doing, greatly improved their public relations in the local community.

The member charged with internal and garden design created a small, English family 'hotel' in a well-planned English garden. Furniture and decorations in the common rooms are provided by the Society, while the residents bring to their private room all furniture except for a bed (special in an Extra Care house—one that can be raised, lowered, and is designed for turning occupants) and a built-in wardrobe. With 23 residents to feed plus on-duty members of a total of 21 staff, and with all the residents' washing to process, the Society found it necessary to buy industrial equipment for the kitchen and laundry.

Activity on the personnel side was initiated long before building completion, with the experience of other Abbeyfield Extra Care houses noted. Visits and inquiries were made, not only into qualifications and training aspects but also with a view to getting the feeling of such work and to study how it could be done while practicing the traditional Abbeyfield concern for the dignity of residents. The house manager or matron (an experienced state registered nurse) was employed some three months before opening day. This enabled her to get to know the Society, the area, and the future residents, and thus to be prepared for a calm reception to the first residents on day one.

The Sub-committee member in charge of personnel, now with a companion volunteer, and later joined by the house manager elect, had also started to work with the Society's organizing secretary on assessing and selecting the first Extra Care residents. Their policy was to give priority to Supportive house residents in Cambridge but in the likely event that the house could not be filled from these, to invite applicants from other Abbeyfield Societies, after which the main vacancies would be filled from the outside world. The Supportive residents and their relatives were given the chance to see the house before it was finally finished so that they could have time for reflection. All residents were admitted during the first four days after opening. It was felt that no protracted staging was advisable for fear of creating spurious seniorities. Only two of the residents who have left, left before their natural end, which occurred after devoted terminal care.

The building design was based on a 'cruciform' layout, providing good communications, a center close to all rooms, good views for all rooms, good circulation and distribution routes, ease of administration, and a family atmosphere, not an institutional one. However, the design provided too small an office for the manager and deputy manager, and the Society made insufficient use both of a short stay room and a smaller living room, so turned them into residents' rooms, raising capacity to 23 with favorable effects on financial viability. It is easy to judge errors in hindsight but there can be no recriminations if the best possible decisions are made on the information available at the time. Of course the best judges are the residents themselves, but it is a brave society who asks have they got it right!

Doctors, a chiropodist, and a hairdresser all call weekly or as required. Volunteers operate a mini shop on wheels which visits all residents twice a week. Activities are encouraged such as art classes and reading groups, and a physiotherapist has regular exercise classes in the living room. Wheelchairs and walking frames abound but this does not stop the residents being taken out in groups for 'treats'. Voluntary services, including transport, are always sought but if not available the Society will bring them in to improve the quality of life of its residents.

Conclusion

The Abbeyfield concept of care for older people is unique in being initiated, developed, and managed by volunteers of diverse expertise who come together to provide the needed housing and care for older people in their common community. The work of providing housing and care are thus spread so that no one is overly burdened by costs or tasks, and all contribute what they can to support each house: volunteers and staff, the support of the Abbeyfield National Society and government aid for older people, and the residents and their families and friends in the community. The co-operative spirit that fuels the effort is the foundation for the 'family' atmosphere that is the key to the happiness of the residents, and sets Abbeyfield houses apart from either solitary living in a house or apartment, or managed care in a nursing home. The balance between privacy and companionship, and between independence and support, ensures that Abbeyfield residents retain their dignity as they grow older.

The Guiding Principles of the Abbeyfield Society describe the respect and care for older people that motivates members of Abbeyfield, and provides a structural guide for the success of Abbeyfield houses. The rapid growth of Abbeyfield Societies and houses in the UK and in ten countries around the world proves its viability and its adaptability to diverse geographical, cultural, and economic situations. Abbeyfield serves a special group of people, those single and older who are unwilling or unable to live alone. Its basic principles, however, embody a balance of privacy and sharing, of volunteer and paid work, and creative co-operation within the community that make the Abbeyfield concept of care unique.

APPENDIX A

THE GUIDING PRINCIPLES OF ABBEYFIELD

THE ABBEYFIELD SOCIETY, founded as an expression of Christian concern for older people, is a co-operative effort by people of faith and goodwill.

Members of the Abbeyfield Society believe:

that older people have an important role to play amongst their families, friends and community;

secondly, that many older people suffer from loneliness and insecurity;

and thirdly, that within the community the individual has an essential part to play in helping older people in special need.

THE SOCIETY'S PURPOSE, therefore, is to provide older people with their own homes within the security and companionship of small households, which can become focal points for goodwill and friendly contact within the community.

THE FOLLOWING PATTERN has been evolved to achieve this purpose.

(a) in all areas wherever there is a need a local Abbeyfield Society is set up which will have full local responsibility for opening and maintaining Abbeyfield houses;

(b) houses are situated in the communities from which the residents are usually drawn;

(c) loneliness is the primary consideration in the selection of residents;

(d) residents have rooms of their own, furnish them as they wish and look after them;

(e) the privacy of each resident's room is respected, but visits from relations, friends and neighbours are encouraged;

(f) each resident pay his or her share of the running costs of the house;

(g) a housekeeper residing in each house cares for the residents, runs the house and provides and prepares the main meals;

(h) local clergy and ministers are made aware of the house and given the opportunity to visit as in an ordinary home. Any arrangements for services or prayers within the house are made in accordance with the wishes of the residents.

In sharing these beliefs, and following this general pattern of work, local societies achieve the purpose of the Abbeyfield Society.

Notes

1. A Manual of Information on legal and financial items is currently being revised to include information on all matters of interest to Local Societies. Other countries use this information adapted to local conditions. Deisgn standards are defined in special manuals. A price list covering a wide range of items is available on request.

2. The Abbeyfield Profile (produced triannually by Abbeyfield UK)

   Available from: Abbeyfield International
   Abbeyfield House
   53 Victoria Street
   St. Albans
   Hertfordshire AL1 3UW
   England

   Tel: 01727 811454
   01727 846168

3. As the world population ages, there is much work for Abbeyfield Societies to do across the world, trying to help improve the quality of life for older people unwilling or unable to live along. Much has been written about Abbeyfield over the years.

   a) Old Homes—New Families: Shared Housing for the Elderly 1984. Co-author—Gordon F. Streib, Graduate Research Professor of Social Gerontology, University of Florida.

   b) The World Ageing Situation 1991. A United Nations Report.

   c) Independent Review of the Abbeyfield Society (Australia) Ltd—Model of Housing by the Commonwealth Government. May 1991. The conclusion reached was that Abbeyfield was "socially acceptable, cost-effective, and well worth supporting."

   d) Publications of the Abbeyfield Society (UK) include: "This Is Abbeyfield"; "About Abbeyfield"; "Any Questions"; "Introducing Abbeyfield"—a guide for GP's and health professionals. Publications of Abbeyfield International include: "Formation Guidance for Local Groups"; "Some Tried and Tested Methods for the Acquisitions of Abbeyfield Houses across the World"; "Abbeyfield International Review" (annually); "Abbeyfield World" (half-yearly).

CHAPTER 8

Zoning as a Tool for Shared Housing

Patricia Baron Pollak

A shared residence is, in essence, the home of a group of people who wish to live together, in much the same way as traditional family related by blood, marriage, or adoption does. The essential ingredient holding the shared residence together, however, is not the legal/biological bond, but rather the bond formed voluntarily by relationships. In essence, those who come together to share their home and their lives embody many of the same values as a traditional family. They care about one another, they prepare and eat meals together, and they share the responsibilities of running and maintaining a home. The essential difference is that the shared residence 'family' is a voluntary one.

One way that a community can affirm a commitment to 'family values' is through the provisions of its zoning regulations. Permitting those who come together as a 'voluntary' family to live together, in a single home, in the same type of structure, in the same neighborhood as other families related by legal and/or biological bonds is an expression of a policy of inclusion rather than exclusion. It allows people to live together in a supportive environment in the same way that traditional families do. It also requires that the community focus attention on the values it wishes to support.

Zoning for shared residences is an issue of family values. The conceptual framework within which shared residences fit is non-partisan. It is neither liberal nor conservative. It embodies family values because the people who are interested in living in a shared residence are trying to approximate the traditional family as much as anyone. The type of shared residence this chapter focuses on is the group home for well, independent, non-service-dependent elderly people, in a single-family house on a single-family street in any neighborhood. These homes, however, are often prohibited in single-family neighborhoods through provisions of the community's zoning ordinance.

Low density, residential zoning provides economic support for the 'American Dream' of each family owning its own home, where mom stays at home to raise the children and dad goes off to work. If commercial and industrial uses are allowed to compete in the market for land, then in many communities, home ownership would be beyond the financial grasp of most American families. In many communities, after World War II, zoning regulations were developed to protect some land for single-family residential development. Without such protection, business and industry could pay more for land than families. Zoning regulations protect designated residential areas from the possibility of commercial/industrial development by allowing only low-density, family housing to be built.

But a lot has changed since Ozzie Nelson, Donna Reed and Ward and June Cleaver represented families that most Americans found similar to their own. Over the years, this ideal American family has dwindled to encompass a decreasing proportion of the population. According to the Census, in 1950 married couples both with and without children comprised 78 percent of all households. In 1988, this group was almost 57 percent of households, and married couples with children were 27 percent of households. By the mid-1980s, traditional families or married couples with their own children and mom at home, comprised less than nine percent of the population. Single-family zoning, created to support a way of life that no longer describes the way the majority of our population lives today, can be viewed as obsolete.

There are two primary zoning issues that affect shared housing. Both issues concern the regulations that specify or restrict the use of a single-family house. The first is the zoning regulation's definition of the term 'family'. The second is the zoning tradition of regulating land use rather than land users.

Zoning Issues: The Definition of Family

A zoning ordinance's definition of the term "family" places legal restrictions on shared living and also raises questions about the traditional concept of family. For example, though a functional family unit, or "voluntary family", can be simply two people living together in a match-up arrangement, or more people living together in a shared residence, a family may be defined in zoning regulations by the number of unrelated people in the household. A common zoning definition of "family" includes those with a biological or legal relationship, meaning those who are related by blood, marriage or adoption, and frequently limits on the number of otherwise unrelated individuals. Such a definition prohibits a greater number of unrelated people from living together in a shared household. The notion of zoning provisions regulating the relationships of those within a home seems to bear a questionable relationship to zoning's legitimate government purpose of protecting the health, safety, and general welfare of the public. Yet in U.S. communities, single-family zoning favoring the nuclear family is highly treasured, and there is great reluctance to see it compromised.

Historically, few zoning ordinances had any definition of family beyond specifying a single housekeeping unit. More recently, however, members of a number of constituencies have demonstrated a preference for living together in "voluntary families" and have presented themselves as "families" to live in single-family dwellings in single-family zones.[1] Communities have responded by incorporating more specific and restrictive "family definitions" into their zoning ordinances. These ordinances have been legally challenged, generally on the basis of due process and equal protection clauses in state constitutions. (Pollak 1991) Some state constitutions such as California's have a "right to privacy" included.

Often in state court decisions the central issue hinges on whether the court finds a group to be a functional family, what they call "the functional equivalent of a family." Decisions have most often been made on cases where the number of people involved ranged between four and six regardless of the size of the unit or the number of rooms. Court decisions, however, usually stop short of specifying how many people can make up the functional equivalent of a family. Basing a legal number of occupants on the size of a home may sound reasonable at first. How big is the house? How many rooms does it have? It may seem that matching the size of the house and number of rooms to an appropriate number of residents is a logical and fair approach to determine a "family." But envision enforcement. If we limit a two-bedroom house to no more than four occupants, how do we ensure compliance? A mother and father share one bedroom and two children share the second bedroom. Must we then require the code enforcement officer to enforce family planning? If the mother becomes pregnant, do we file charges against the family or threaten eviction? Say: "Since you have a two-bedroom house, with a third child you can't live there anymore." Moreover, if we require the voluntary family to have one person per bedroom, will we do the same for the biological family? Many local governments have passed regulations that set a limit on the number of people who occupy a house based on the size of the unit and number of rooms, but excuse the legal/biological family and not the voluntary family from enforcement. However, some recent state court decisions have required equal treatment of both types of households.[2]

Regulating the number of residents in a single-family house is a complicated and tricky issue, particularly in times when homelessness is an important issue. There may be a point at which a dwelling is no longer a single-family home but is, in fact, an "institution." Yet the essential point seems to be not in regulating occupancy by biological or legal relationship or on an arbitrary number of unrelated residents, but rather in the operation of the home as a functional "family."

Zoning Issues: Regulation of Land Use

It is well established that zoning regulates land use rather than the land user, or occupant. This means that zoning focuses on what the real property is used for, the building on the land. For shared residences, the distinction between land use and land user is crucial. If we consider an existing single-family house, then setbacks, height limits, design features, lot size, lot coverage, placement of the building on the lot, off-street parking, etc. have already been approved. The land use in the zoning district is fixed as residential at a particular density. The only difference for many shared residences, such as those for the elderly, is in the occupancy of a particular house (the land users), and not the use of the land. Few if any of the physical characteristics of the use of the property change with the occupancy of the home. Mom, Dad, and children are replaced by older men and women living as a "voluntary family". The users change, not the use. Nevertheless, through restrictive definitions of family in occupancy requirements, attention to household relationships can be prioritized over zoning's traditional focus on land use. Instead of judging the desirability and acceptability of residential use according to a particular (and increasingly rare) type of social grouping (the nuclear family), we should assess the functional consequences of different kinds of residential families on the land use.

There are many communities that still today consider a functional definition of family inappropriate and insist that areas zoned single-family be occupied by families with legal and biological ties. Many allow households that include a limited number of unrelated people (usually three to four). Some communities are willing to consider raising the number of unrelated individuals who may live together in a single family dwelling if the occupants are "elderly".

The validity of zoning ordinances constructed specifically to allow shared housing for the elderly has been subject to judicial review in several states. In the New York State case of Maldini v. Ambro,[3] the town had zoned for a "Retirement Community District." Opponents argued that the town had exceeded its authority by specifically segregating out a particular class of users. The court decided to uphold the ordinance, stating:

> That the "users" of the retirement community district have been considered in creating a zoning classification does not necessarily render the amendment suspect, nor does it clash with traditional "use" concepts of zoning. Including the needs of potential "users" cannot be disassociated from sensible community planning based on the "use" to which the property is to be put. The line between legitimate and illegitimate exercise of the zoning power cannot be drawn by resort to formula, but as in other areas of the law, will vary with surrounding circumstances and conditions. [4]

So, in Maldini v. Ambro, the designation of a land-user zoning class of "senior citizen" was held as valid. In another case, Campbell v. Barraud,[5] the use of such a zoning class was extended:

> If it is within the zoning power of the town to provide for the special housing needs of the elderly, by accommodations specifically designed to satisfy their economic, physical, psychological and social needs, and the Court of Appeals has held that it is, it must also be permissible for a town board, acting in its legislative capacity, to ensure that such housing is used by the very group for which it has been designed.[6]

In the New Jersey case "Taxpayers Association of Weymouth Township, Inc. v. Weymouth Township",[7] a complaint challenged the validity of ordinances that allowed districts to be created where one of the permitted uses was a mobile home park for the exclusive use of the elderly. The court concluded that housing is a basic need, and that encouraging the provision of shelter through the use of a zoning ordinance legitimately serves the general welfare. Furthermore, the court also ruled that the special physical, financial, social, and psychological needs of the elderly deserve the sort of special consideration the municipality had taken. The municipality had not exceeded its authority.[8]

State judicial review of shared housing provisions remains unfinished. While in many states courts have upheld the concept of zoning for the elderly, this does not mean that courts in other states will concur. However, precedent plays an important role in shaping judicial deliberations. The Maldini Decision in New York and similar decisions in other states improve the likelihood that zoning for the elderly as a specific class of user will pass muster in the courts. Local governments hoping to offer improved housing opportunities for the elderly will likely adopt many of the court approved provisions in their own zoning ordinances and so allow for and encourage shared housing, accessory apartments, or cottages for the elderly that will withstand legal challenge.

As time passes, litigation surrounding the Federal Fair Housing Amendments Act of 1988 continues to address that law's application to municipal zoning and how those designated "handicapped" will fare. The new amendments to the Federal Fair Housing Law define handicaps broadly. The law states that not only should those judged handicapped be treated like those who are not, but that governments should make "reasonable accommodation" available to the handicapped. This may mean that local government would require housing improvements (e.g., changing building codes to require door handles versus knobs, ramps versus steps, and so forth) that improve the accessibility of housing for handicapped residents throughout their jurisdiction or within designated areas. Should the courts determine that the physical, economic, social, and psychological needs of the elderly (already recognized by some courts as a reasonable basis for designating shared housing zones) represent handicaps under the Federal Fair Housing Act, then the provisions of the law might extend to the elderly as well. This federal law would pre-empt local authority, not only making community-by-community litigation unnecessary, but allowing a "voluntary family" of elderly to share housing by right.

Conclusion

Shared housing has great potential to support the lives of those involved and to enrich the array of lifestyles within our communities. Consider the values sustained by shared residences functioning as family households: companionship, mutual respect, caring, concern for one another's well-being. Acceptance of the concept of shared housing requires people to change beliefs and attachments that promote the nuclear family at the expense of other types of families. Local elected officials and citizens often consider such changes in the context of land use and zoning disputes, disputes that too often frame the options as mutually exclusive and antagonistic. Differences in family functions and activity are exaggerated and important similarities overlooked. Judicial review of some of the more persistent litigants in these disputes has so far tended to balance differences and similarities. For instance, the elderly are a kind of family, but a family with special needs.

Zoning permits or prohibits the housing opportunities that are available not only to the elderly, but also to others. Careful amendments to the zoning ordinance, such as a generic "functional equivalent of a family" occupancy requirement, can acknowledge the changes in family composition and permit housing opportunities that will fairly and efficiently accommodate not only households of the elderly, but a variety of other families as well. Zoning laws that work well fit function to place rather than place to people. Separating family values from a particular form of household structure represents a crucial distinction in the effort to make room for shared housing arrangements. Households may include an unfamiliar mix of people, but behave in familiar ways.

Notes

1. These include college students, young adults, developmentally disabled adults, the elderly, and others.
2. See, for example, McMinn v. Town of Oyster Bay. 1985. 488 N.E. 2d 1240 (N.Y.)
3. 330 N.E. ed 403 (N.Y. 1975), cert. denied, 423 U.S. 993 (1975).
4. 330 N.E. 2d at 407–408.
5. 394 N.Y.S. 2d 909 (N.Y. App. Div. 1977).
6. Id. at 912.
7. 364 A. 2d 1016 (N.J. 1976).
8. Id. at 1028–30.
9. Oxford house-C, et al., v. City of St. Louis. U.S. District Court of Eastern Missouri, 28 January, 1994.

CHAPTER 9

The Trouble with Sharing

Peter Marris

Some years ago I made a study of the development of African businesses in Kenya. One man told me he had formed a partnership early in his career with eleven other businessmen to run a hotel and bar, but they had no concept of how the partnership would work. Their initial idea was that each of them would run the bar for a month and take all the profits, and then hand it over to the next person who would run it for a month and take all the profits. It did not take them very long to discover that this is not an effective way of running a business, since it deprived anyone of the incentive to restock the shelves. The idea of a business partnership, so familiar to us, was unknown and baffling to them. Sharing, I think, always implies a context of established cultural and social expectations. We have tended to idealize sharing, particularly in the 60s and in the early 70s, as part of the counter-cultural rebellion against competitive capitalism, when communes came to symbolize a radical alternative to the military industrial complex. Communes—or at least some of them—implied a total relationship in an unselfish, spontaneous setting without private ownership or individualistic contracts. But an enormous amount of time, energy, and emotional effort had then to be absorbed in constantly trying to constitute and reconstitute the relationships of the group. Sharing is not a spontaneous, simple or easily managed relationship. In the pages which follow, I try to explore what the success of sharing depends on, and then relate that to housing. I am not, in any sense, an expert on shared housing. (I studied some issues of housing in Africa, very little in this country.) What I have to say is of a more general and theoretical nature.

Sharing, like any other human relationship, depends upon trust and predictability. All human relationships require predictability; if they are not predictable we cannot handle them. You have to know how someone

115

can be expected to behave towards you. You have to know what the signals of their behavior and conversation mean in order to be able to respond to them in a meaningful way and manage the relationship. Years ago, Harold Garfinkel, a sociologist at UCLA, invited his students, as an experiment, to contradict everyday expectations of relationships in some quite trivial way (Garfinkel 1967). For instance, if someone was to ask "Can you tell me the time?", you would answer "Yes" and then stop. Or you would ask a bus driver "Does this bus go down Morgan Street?", and the bus driver would say "Yes", and then you would say "But how do you know?"—little things designed simply to disconcert people by not fulfilling their expectations.

Not surprisingly, I think, this behavior very rapidly upset the people upon whom it was practiced. One of the students who carried the experiment out on his wife nearly provoked a divorce. Indeed, even after he had explained that this was simply an experiment that his professor had asked him to undertake, an uneasiness remained. It created a degree of uncertainty in the relationship, a lingering doubt that continued to be troubling.

All relationships, I would argue, depend upon reliable expectations, and we have behaviors that we bring to play when our expectations are not met. Ultimately, all relationships of trust and confidence depend upon the ability to use sanctions against non-compliance. Sanctions may take the form of punishment, ostracism, therapy or emotional withdrawal. Usually, we are prepared to place our trust in relationships only if we feel confident that we can, in the last resort, bring sanctions to bear. For instance—to return a moment to the African businessmen—their progress was constantly hampered by their inability to trust either their customers or their employees. They could not take legal action against defaulters without deeply offending their community, for whom the court system was an alien, colonial intrusion. Yet tradition provided no standards by which to judge conduct in modern business relationships, nor customs by which to regulate it. By contrast, the East African Indian minority had created a very successful wholesale and retail network, because there were few opportunities outside each community's commercial niche, and ostracism was therefore a powerful sanction (Marris and Somerset 1971; Marris 1961).

Any kind of relationship requires explicit, defined expectations, mutual agreement and effective sanctions. Without that, the relationship has to be continually renegotiated and discussed. This becomes enormously time-consuming, because if nothing can be taken for granted, every encounter, in a sense, has to be redefined and renegotiated. Consider, for instance, the contrast between courtship and marriage. Courtship can be an enormously time-consuming relationship. Neither one knows quite what to expect of the other. They are interested, but they are afraid of making commitments that may lead them to be hurt afterwards. They do not know what the behavior of the other person means, so they themselves are alternately welcoming and defensive toward the relationship. That behavior, in turn, creates confusion for the other person. There is a period, I think, in many courtships when there is a great deal of anxiety and an enormous amount of uncertainty, and the relationship absorbs all your energy. Then there is a point at which the relationship comes to be defined. Either it is "on" or it is "off". Once it is "on" and it is defined as being "on", then expectations begin to be formed which enable the relationship to become somewhat routinized. The object of marriage, in a way, is to routinize the relationship so that people can get on with their lives.

To come now back to housing. When we share a house, we typically share space, tasks, time and sometimes costs; sometimes also food. Most people live most of their lives sharing housing with others, usually members of their family—husbands and wives and children, if no one else. It is worth thinking about how we do even that, which is not necessarily simple or without conflict and tension. How does a family share? Typically, a family tries not to have to share too much. Everybody has their own room, if possible. Certainly the parents have a bedroom, separate from the children's bedroom/s, if they can. Nor do we usually share a lot of tasks. In a co-operative household where the husband does a half share, he does not usually do that half share by cooking the evening meal together with his wife. Rather, he cooks one night and the wife another. We tend to divide tasks—he takes the garbage out, she does the shopping. Even if there is no gender division of labor, we are likely to suggest "you do it one night, I'll do it the next night." The members of the household have different tasks on different days, integrated with the different timetables of each person's life—getting to work, getting to school, to exercise class . . .

The way an ordinary family manages to share is, then, paradoxically by not having to share too much, but rather by sharing out. The areas of conflict tend to be precisely those things which you cannot share out. If the household has only one television set, then that is where the conflict is going to be: who gets to watch what program, when. And bathrooms. As families grow more prosperous, they typically build more bathrooms, buy more television sets, and build more rooms, so that they do not have to share.

The same principle, by the way, is apparent in the more egalitarian societies of East Africa. Despite the idealization of a spirit of community in modern conceptions of African socialism, traditional African societies such as the Kikuyu shared out far more than they shared. Each son, when he married, was allotted his own land; in a polygamous household, each wife with her children had her own hut, her own fields. The crucial difference between such a system and our own lies not in what is shared, but the distinction between ownership and rights of use. Land, in Kikuyu East Africa, belonged to a kinship group, ultimately to a clan; membership in a kin group constituted a right to claim use of a piece of that land. We have individualized ownership. But still, at the scale of the family, much the same distinction applies: the family owns the house, while each member of the family can claim rights of use. Shared housing—as distinct from the single family house—is unusual essentially because individuals who would not normally be associated together in this way jointly own a property for their own use. Given that, the need to share out space, and to regulate the rights and duties of each member in regard to common rooms and facilities, is essentially the same.

None of this is simple. It is arrived at by a process of negotiation and routinization. And of course it is also reinforced by a great many shared expectations. But even in the most loving and best run of families, expectations are not always met or indeed mutually understood, and then sanctions are brought into play. The sanctions are usually the withdrawal, in some way or another, of intimacy, love and comfort or companionship— the things that people seek from their relationship with each other. It is either emotional withdrawal, coldness, or if the transgression is serious and it does not get resolved, then it may become a threat of separation. There are very powerful sanctions behind the everyday negotiated compromises and agreements of a household's everyday life. Usually mild sanctions are enough. A little coldness, a little indifference, a little going off on your own is enough to bring about first of all concern, then gestures of apology. Then often, if the marriage relationship is a good one, the couple will discuss how the quarrel arose, and renegotiate some aspect of their relationship.

To say that people on the whole try not to share more than they can— they share out more than they share—is not to say that there is a lack of real love and affection and companionship. I am not trying to say that we are all such self-centered individualists that the only way that we can live together is by having our private rooms. I think it is something different, an aspect of the egalitarianism of American society. In other societies the same kinds of problems may be dealt with in a much more authoritarian way: for instance when a patriarch regulates relationships. Then sharing can be imposed on people, and they have to make the best of it. The junior wife in a traditional Yoruba family compound ranked lowest in a hierarchy of authority reaching up to the senior male, and could claim very little for herself. But if you want to make sharing a more mutually agreeable relationship, something more egalitarian, you have to find that delicate balance where people feel safe that they can engage in intimate relationships with others without their autonomy being overwhelmed.

This connection between autonomy and space has been an enduring theme in the struggle for equality for women, from Catharine Beecher's An American Woman's Home to Virginia Woolf's A Room of One's Own. Beecher idealized the role of wife and mother, conceiving the kitchen as the central command post from which she could supervise all the activities of the household. The home was both her machine and the symbolic expression of her values. But Beecher's paragon of domestic efficiency and moral inspiration had no place to be herself. She was absorbed in her role as the "minister of the home church of Jesus Christ." In the face of these cultural prescriptions, Woolf's call for a room of one's own represents a radical assertion of a woman's right to nurture her own self, as well as her family. Yet, at the same time, a parallel theme in the history of women's struggle has been the promotion of shared facilities—day nurseries, community kitchens, and laundries (Hayden 1981: 56). While prosperous families may add more rooms, they rarely add more kitchens, largely because it would be both lonely and wasteful of time and effort if members of the household cooked separate meals. The "material feminists" argued that it was almost as lonely, and equally wasteful, for each family to cook for itself. Though their vision has been replaced by fast food restaurants, laundromats, and child care centers, the principle remains: for practical reasons, as well as companionship, we want to share, and yet we do not want to have to share some things ever, almost nothing all the time. How these issues are worked out will vary with the class, culture and resources of the household. A Chicano family in East Los Angeles will use the spaces of a typical Southern California bungalow differently from a family in Korea Town or Santa Monica. The arrangement of domestic space both reflects and reinforces the balance of power that allocates the pleasures, rights, and duties of nurturing and self-fulfillment, companionship and privacy.

Sharing between people who are not part of the same family, and perhaps not even part of the same household, raises the same issues of how mutual obligations and privacy can be balanced and protected. But now the sanctions against non-compliance are likely to be weaker, because both the emotional and financial interdependence are typically more casual and expedient. Breaking up the household is less threatening. The sharers may also be more alike. If two adults of the same sex are sharing a house—two single mothers, for instance—they are more likely to want to do the same things, at the same time—cook, or bathe the baby—than a husband and wife. Thus the problems of sharing are compounded, and the sanctions are weaker. So it seems to me that successful sharing depends on one of two things: either very strong social sanctions against nonconforming behavior, or explicit rules to follow, as in a monastic order. Sharing works in a monastic order because of the commitment of everybody in their society to a set of principles and ideals, which are usually highly structured and authoritatively imposed. The Shaker village in Hancock, Massachusetts, is a beautifully articulated set of shared spaces, architecturally plain, but perfectly proportioned. It worked because of the strict codes of behavior—including even posture and body movements—which the Shaker religion enjoined on its members.

I suggest, then, that all relationships of sharing require authoritative codes of conduct, reinforced by effective sanctions; and to reduce the risks of conflict, and the effort of continual responsiveness to the behavior of others in any but the most routinized situations, it is often better to share out resources rather than to share them. The greater the range of values and conduct permitted in a society, the more variable the patterns of interdependence, and the more egalitarian the relationships between the sharers, the more demanding sharing becomes. Clarity of expectations, regulation and sharing out are more than ever crucial. And there is another factor, which I believe also particularly influences the viability of shared housing: the size of the market. If people who want a particular kind of shared relationship have available to them a sufficiently large number of opportunities to enter into that relationship, they can look again if any particular relationship does not work out. Consider, for instance, college dormitories and college roommates. You have two or three people who are not related to each other living together perhaps a year or two at a time, with often little or no private space, and dependent on each other to keep the place reasonably tidy, to accommodate each others friends, and to enable each other to get some work done. The system works partly because around the university there is a big market in roommates. If you do not get on with your roommate, you can negotiate something else with somebody else. This also means you can push people out if you do not get on, or you can leave. So there is an "out" that enables you to try that relationship again with others.

There is also, within the university, a tradition of that kind of sharing. People have some sense of what problems may arise, how you negotiate them, which problems have to be accepted and negotiated, what behavior is so outrageous that you should not have to put up with it, and so on.

Given all these conditions—a society that understands and knows how to regulate forms of sharing, and provides opportunities for it—the success of shared housing will still, of course, be much influenced by its design. How public and private spaces are joined, and mediated by transitional spaces such as porches or yards where people can interact without crossing the boundary between private and public, how privacy and supervision balance to combine safety with freedom, has been researched by Clare Cooper, Kathryn McCamant, Charles Durrett and Dolores Hayden, amongst others (Cooper, Marcus and Sarkissian 1986; McCamant and Durrett 1988; Hayden 1984). I will not attempt to summarize their findings here. But, obviously enough, refining design to accommodate sharing depends upon opportunities to build it.

In the United States, many kinds of sharing that are potentially desirable and convenient turn out to be illegal. Residential zoning regulations typically forbid accessory apartments, mixed business and domestic use, renting out rooms, and even the occupation of single-family dwellings by households of unrelated members. This illegality is related to the perpetuation of the single-family house as not simply a social ideal, but even more importantly, as an investment. This is a peculiarity of modern western societies—the extent to which the exchange value of a house has come to determine its use.

In feudal society, real property—real estate—was distinguished from personal property because it could not, unlike personal property, be freely bought, sold or willed. Only with the rise of an urban, merchant, middle-class did the distinction begin to disappear, gradually assimilating all land titles to a conception of land as an exchangeable commodity like any other. In a capitalist society, as Henri Lefebvre argues (trans. 1991), space becomes redesigned and reorganized to facilitate its sale. And what makes a commodity readily saleable and readily marketable is, he suggests, its standardization. Each unit is comparable to other units and therefore can be readily priced. The characteristic grid plan of American cities, for instance, divides space up into equivalent squares that can then be priced. It becomes much more difficult to deal with space as a marketable commodity if each lot and each building is very different from every other one. Mortgage banks will avoid or deliberately undervalue unusual properties because they do not know what to compare them to.

Home owners, once they have their mortgage in hand, are drawn into complicity with these rules of assessment, for fear of compromising their investment. Any change in the composition of the neighborhood is liable to have an unpredictable effect on values, and therefore to be threatening. The kind of person who would buy a house as a single-family residence is, arguably, of a different social class, age group, and perhaps race than those who would buy it to share. These newcomers might well enhance property values, but in the face of uncertainty, home owners as much as banks are likely to resist any accommodation with changing household structures, populations, and tastes. So there are political as well as institutionalized constraints perpetuating the idea that the single-family house is the only marketable form of dwelling.

A friend bought a house in Los Angeles a few years ago, for instance, with a rented unit in the bottom. This was one of the reasons why he was attracted to the house—the income from the rented unit paid a large part of the mortgage. (The unit was of course illegal, as these things usually are.) But as a condition of a mortgage, the bank he approached wanted to remove the kitchen from the basement floor—which he had rather neatly disguised as a studio. What sense does that make? If he did not rent it out, it reduced the value of the property, and reduced his ability to afford it. Nonetheless, from the bank's point of view this was an anomaly that somehow made the building less lendable.

Another less trivial example: some years ago an architect was involved in designing some low-cost, low-income units of housing in Los Angeles in the Willowbrook area, that were to be partly financed by a hospital and partly by a foundation. The idea was to produce housing for single mothers with a lot of shared facilities including a child care center. As the design progressed two things happened. First of all, the child care center, which had been placed at the back so it would face onto the shared space where it was quietest, was moved to the main road at the front, because the hospital wanted people to see the good that they were doing for the community and they wanted credit for this. But secondly, the participating bank would not lend on the project as an integrated design. It insisted on the child care center being split-off as a separate project, with a separate mortgage, so that the two now were not an integrated property but two separate properties. Even with money and institutional backing and a sensitive design that reflected much thought about issues of sharing and what single mothers needed, the project was seriously compromised, and took many years to complete.

I have argued that sharing is an inherently complex relationship, dependent upon the regulation of mutual expectations, on culture, on sanctions, on features of design; that it is not an easy relationship at the best of times or a natural one; it has to be thought about, created, and carefully articulated. There are institutional barriers as well as cultural barriers in the United States to creating these kinds of conditions. But there are compelling rewards to sharing, too—companionship, relief from isolation, access to amenities we could not afford for ourselves. Ideally, I suggest, each of us should be able to enjoy three kinds of spaces: private space, where we can take refuge from the constraints, conflicts, and effort of human interaction; public space, where we can enjoy company and resources beyond our individual means; and in-between spaces, where we can feel connected without being fully committed to the public world. These last are some of the most enjoyable places of all—porches, balconies, sidewalk cafe tables. And our right to enjoy all such places needs to be recognized, respected, and protected.

But far too many of us are denied the opportunity—even the right—to enjoy any of these kinds of spaces. The homeless are chivvied from shelter to shelter, desperately trying to cling to a car, a locker, a suitcase they can call their own, without any refuge from the relentless rules of human interaction, even as they try to sleep. (Liebow 1993) For many the stoops and hallways and shared yards that once facilitated an unintrusive neighborly sociability and mutual support have become too dangerous to inhabit. Everywhere, people are retreating fearfully from public places. We are turning what ought to be public—the street, the park—into private enclaves behind gates and guards, and we are turning what ought to be private into public shame, denying the least fortunate even the minimum refuge for their dignity and repose. If we are to recover or reinvent the conditions which make the sharing of space companionable and convenient, we also need to reinvent the spaces which we should not have to share—to make available to everyone, whatever their resources, a space of their own, where they can be themselves. And paradoxically, perhaps, I think it is to this last ideal that experiments in shared housing have most to contribute.

CHAPTER 10

Conclusion

Shared Housing Meets Special Needs

Shared housing responds directly to the housing needs of people for whom conventional housing proves inadequate. Some groups fit the stereotype of the needy dependent: poor and low-income families and single adults, teen-aged mothers with children, and service-dependent persons. But these people's sharing does not simply reflect passive accommodation to necessity. They actively carve out common social and physical space that not only provides shelter, but social and economic support as well, while maintaining privacy and autonomy for the household. Many middle-class households also possess housing needs best met by sharing, including: people who need or want to work at home, elderly seeking companionship and mutual aid, as well as those seeking to create alternative residential communities based on voluntary reciprocity rather than kinship.

In its variety of forms, shared housing supports the capacity to respond to critically changed circumstances in people's lives, such as caring for an elderly parent, losing income, having a child, or coping with disability. The diverse types of shared housing encourage social reciprocity, whether based primarily on mutual dependence, a desire for companionship, mutual caring, or some mix. Thus sharing, while often an accommodation to necessity, is a purposeful and voluntary effort to collaborate with others in meeting the changing demands of everyday life. Sharing bridges the commodity gap between human needs and consumer goods through reduced rent, more efficient use of appliances, energy conservation, and so forth.

Each shared housing situation has unique characteristics reflecting the circumstances and the setting. However, there are clear commonalities and differences which suggest general kinds of shared housing based on the purposes of sharing: household situations; special populations; and life style choices.

125

Sharing that is responsive to household situations includes the often temporary responses to changes in financial, employment, and health conditions and other personal crises. It also includes the more long term situations of low-income, single-parent, and other families who have difficulty managing their households alone. Ahrentzen offers several examples of transitional housing that enables teen-aged mothers and single-parent families to care for their children and receive needed support for themselves: to go to school, to obtain counselling and job training, to provide child care. These examples vary widely in site, scale, design, and organization in responding to residents' needs for different degrees of community support, services, and independence. Hemmens and Hoch describe how some homeowners in poor neighborhoods share their homes with extended family and friends who are in emergency need, who are or become dependent on others for care, or to accommodate reordered social relationship resulting from migration, displacement, or abandonment.

Shared housing that serves the needs of special populations, such as the elderly, single-parent families, home-based workers, or homeless, can provide an environment, services, and resources targeted to support their specific needs. Such housing can increase access to amenities and resources that individual households cannot afford, as well as services, such as the counselling provided at Lakefront SRO Corporation's buildings or job training at Warren Village in Denver. As Biddlecombe and Pollak describe, loneliness, increasing physical frailty, and a fixed income can make living alone impractical and unaffordable for the elderly. An increasing variety of shared housing options have been developed that the elderly can use to retain an autonomous foothold in their neighborhood: remodelled single-family homes, accessory apartments and elder cottages, match-up agreements, and group homes like Abbeyfield helps produce. Similarly, group homes in residential settings provide a high quality environment for persons of varying abilities who need the services of assisted living.

Sharing that reflects life style choice includes both social and economic purposes. A growing number of people who could afford to live in single-family detached houses choose to live in shared housing. Ahrentzen and Leavitt relate examples of younger middle to upper-income households who custom-build shared homes to fit their work-at-home and social contact needs, or who join in cohousing collectives. These households choose sharing less for reasons of economic need than the desire to belong to a community where residents know each other and all pitch in together to make the daily tasks of household management less burdensome. Several chapters include examples of the economic function of shared housing. The typically lower rents free a greater proportion of income for other needs, in-kind arrangements secure housing for those without cash resources, and renting out an extra room can be a source of income for the homeowner. As Hardman shows, broad demographic changes are producing demands for a more flexible use of existing housing stock. The number of nuclear households has been on the decline for decades. The structure of most households currently does not match the independent nuclear family for whom the one house—one family ideal has been upheld.

The need for social interaction and the ability to share successfully cuts across income, age, and ethnic or racial groups. Several authors agree on the need for social contact among poor and disadvantaged households, especially in transitional and public housing developments, to counteract the isolation and lack of self-esteem stemming from "lower" social status and limited opportunities for economic improvement. Similarly, the provision of group homes, mother-in-law apartments, and other non-traditional housing in residential areas meets the needs of many to maintain their individual relationships, and fosters an enriching social environment.

Critical Differences in Sharing

Shared housing differs from conventional housing because the member households structure the relationship between private and public responsibilities mainly by negotiated social agreements and consensus rather than legal relationships of ownership, family and tenancy. However, people who prefer the pleasures of sharing to those of possession find themselves at a significant disadvantage. Housing policy, finance, and regulation all support single-family home ownership.

The people and policies that organize conventional housing markets believe strongly in the efficacy and virtue of one family – one house. The popularity of this belief, however, imposes burdens on those households unable or unwilling to purchase a single-family house. It is thought, though seldom stated, that if possession of a house by a single-family supposedly ensures security, order, and prosperity, then shared housing among several households must bring uncertainty, crime, and poverty. And if the benefits of single-family housing are to shine brightly, then the benefits of shared housing must be kept hidden in the shadows. The standard of the single-family house, and its hold on the expectations of builders, realtors, bankers, public officials, and owners, severely restricts the use of the single-family housing stock and limits opportunities to build new designs to accommodate the needs of non-nuclear households. Zoning and subdivision regulations implemented to protect the individual homeowner from incompatible land uses and substandard developments prohibit most forms of shared housing. In common agreement, developers negotiate with local planning staff and elected officials to produce segmented, stratified homogeneous subdivisions.

Over the past several decades there has been significant erosion in the practical realization of the single-family house ideal. Rising land costs, construction costs, changing demographics, and other factors have resulted in the housing of a large and growing percentage of the population in condominiums and common interest developments (CIDs), as discussed in the Introduction. While these housing forms retain the single-family house character of ownership and exclusive use, it is limited to the inside of the structure actually inhabited by the household. Usually control over and ownership of building exterior and exterior space are placed with a homeowners association. The differences between such developments and the kinds of shared housing discussed in this book make clear the continuing importance of the single-family house ideal in determining what is acceptable housing and development policy.

What is shared in CIDs and condominiums is ownership, use and management of outdoor space, external building surfaces, and interior space devoted to circulation and utilities. What is not shared is interior living space. The spaces for dining, cooking, and leisure are not shared. Condominiums often have a 'party room', but its main use is reserved for private parties of individual households. Similarly, there seldom is sharing of outside activities such as gardening. Typically, each household may have a small private outdoor space which they manage and use privately, but the majority of outdoor space is managed by the association for the individual use of the resident households. Joint use of outdoor space is considered acceptable, but collective use of interior space for routine, essential household activities is not. The housing units may be under one roof or attached, but they operate as free-standing units to the extent possible. In this way the myth of single-family housing is maintained in structures that do not resemble the single-family house ideal.

Arguments Against the Stigma of Shared Housing

The practical concern behind the attachment of most households to the single-family house neighborhood is their concern that mixing in other uses such as shared housing will reduce the value of their property. Since the house is the single largest investment of most households and their principal store of wealth, hedge against inflation, and hope for eventual financial gain, this is a reasonable concern. But the available evidence does not support the concern that shared housing will necessarily reduce the value of nearby single-family residences.

Ahrentzen uses the example of high-income condominium development across the street from Warren Village to show that transitional shared housing does not necessarily devalue adjacent property. Butzen makes the case that the high quality rehabilitation work involved in developing Lakefront's SRO buildings actually increased adjacent property values. She emphasizes though, that it was efforts to build good community relations with neighbors that proved critical to Lakefront's success.

Shared housing schemes for middle and upper-income persons, such as the GoHomes that provide shared work and living space in visually attractive buildings, face fewer obstacles than those settlements composed of poor households. Ironically, in some cases, successful development of middle-income shared housing in an aging urban area may contribute to gentrification that displaces lower income residents, as condominium conversion of older apartment buildings did in many cities during the 1970s and is now doing again.

A second argument for repealing the stigma against shared housing is that practical realization of the American housing dream has changed. The single-family house on an individual lot is no longer possible or even desirable for many who could in previous decades have expected to attain it. This argument has several parts. As Hardman and others make clear, the changing demographics of the American population show that there will be increasing numbers of non-traditional households for whom the single-family house is not ideal. The rising costs of urban land that were so important to the growth of CIDs will continue to be a problem for all kinds of residential development, as will rising construction costs. The potential for economies in housing through shared housing offers one, limited remedy both for provision of affordable housing and for maintaining high quality middle-income housing as in the Bainbridge Island cohousing.

A third argument for shared housing is that it increases the choices available to housing consumers. For some there are many disadvantages to living in suburban single-family detached housing: isolation from neighbors, enforced conformity with neighborhood appearance, high mortgage and tax rates, high maintenance costs, auto dependence and income, race and age-related segregation. Many single-family housing residents pay excessive psychic, social, and economic costs for a lifestyle that does not fit their needs. For these people shared housing may offer a useful and valuable option. Such sharing involves voluntary consent and free choice; but freedom to choose is now greatly constrained by the stigma against shared housing.

A fourth argument against current attitudes and policy is that shared housing contributes positively to the development and maintenance of social and economic community rather than disrupting and reducing it. Shared housing involves mutual responsibility among household members and between households. The homeowners in Hemmens and Hoch's study of informal help reported how family responsibilities, emotional attachments, and moral convictions motivated them to share their homes with others. This sharing is based less on altruism than on a sense of obligation to support those in need, expecting the recipients to eventually reciprocate. The expectation of family and community reciprocity provides a powerful source of social stability in a context of changing economic circumstances.

Shared housing residents make and maintain a variety of reciprocal agreements that guide not only the use of common space, but the provision of child care, preparation of meals, care for the sick, celebrations, and other social activities. Organizing and managing situations of social reciprocity is not easy. Marris describes the significant negotiations and difficulties inherent in sharing relationships. Shared housing does not so much outweigh these difficulties as offer social agreements and physical designs for anticipating and coping with these conflicts. The point is not to place shared housing on a pedestal of social harmony, but to acknowledge, identify, and study the sorts of private wants and social needs that shared housing arrangements might usefully meet better than conventional housing.

For many, shared housing appears unattractive because they imagine losing private control over residential space to others. But shared housing does not pose a basic threat to private space. Shared housing simply shifts the boundary between private and public: instead of privacy starting at the lot line, it starts at the door of the private dwelling. Even the largest and wealthiest suburban homeowner must negotiate agreements with neighbors. The shared housing resident does too, only the neighbors share the same roof rather than the same street or subdivision.

Shared housing for the vulnerable and the poor may have the indirect effect of reducing the burden of public service agencies. Lakefront SRO Corporation and other non-profit housing providers provide on-site social services for residents. The households in Hemmens and Hoch's study help each other far more than they receive help from formal helping agencies. Abbeyfield houses rely on neighborhood initiative and local volunteer efforts for general oversight, maintenance, fund-raising, and sharing social relationships among elderly residents. Leavitt argues that work places designed into public housing developments, encouraging residents to provide goods and services according to their skills, increase income and self-sufficiency for residents who have few options. Warren Village has had a significant number of residents who became employed as a result of on-site social services and were then able to maintain individual accom-modations. As Marris points out, enabling poor and homeless people to live in substantial, permanent housing means safer, better public spaces for all as well as protecting the rights of the poor and homeless to privacy.

Characterizing shared housing on a community scale involves more than financial, regulatory, and design interests. Hemmens and Hoch's study suggests that shared housing reinforces family and community values and contributes to neighborhood stability through the ability to share housing with those who could not otherwise remain in their home area. Abbeyfield houses, Biddlecombe writes, benefit the neighborhood in maintaining existing social networks between the elderly residents and their friends and relatives. As well as sharing within the Abbeyfield house, many elderly residents continue to be involved in the daily like of the surrounding community by volunteering to help others through teaching in schools, caring for children, or participating in a variety of informal helping networks.

An Agenda for Research and Policy

Homes collect and locate the results of a variety of policies and practices as they affect people's lives. In homes and among households, these policies and practices are interpreted, maintained, challenged, clarified; they fulfill or disappoint the intentions behind their rules; they hurt or help. People relate to society out of their homes, in working, playing, shopping, voting, visiting, collaborating, learning and teaching, sustaining the fabric of neighborhoods, cultures and the larger society. Limitations on the opportunity for people to share housing, for designers to implement designs specifically for different types of sharing, and for housing providers to finance well-designed, well-run shared housing reduce the capacity for people to respond and adapt to changing economic, social or physical conditions.

Four issues—values, design, regulation, and finance—show up repeatedly as the main concerns for research and policy development on shared housing. These issues interrelate in complex ways. Local regulation of housing and development is ultimately determined to a large extent by values. But these local regulations are also influenced by the lending policies of local financial institutions, which in turn are guided in part by federal housing policy, especially that concerned with mortgage insurance and secondary market operations. Design too is largely controlled by prevailing values and financial policy and practice. To a lesser extent design is constrained, rather than driven, by local regulation. If we put it together, values are at the center of the pattern that supports the current treatment of shared housing. Values in turn influence financial practices and local regulations, with financial practices further influencing local regulations. Housing design, on the edge of the pattern, responds to values, financial practices, and local regulations.

Thus changing the treatment of shared housing requires a change in values. A difficulty emerges, however, in that experience is the most likely source of value change. In this case people need to see and experience shared housing in their communities. The problem, then, is how to generate innovative shared housing developments so that design responsive to people's needs is able to influence values, finance, and regulation.

VALUES

In recent years there has been much national policy discussion about "family values". These values include the transmission of culture, support, help and companionship, the glue of shared experience, formation of public and private identity, the work of learning respect and dignity. These values are shaped in a wider social context as well as in the home. However, housing—where, how much, what type, how it is designed, how it functions—is integral to supporting this important aspect of life in addition to physical shelter.

Typically the idea of family in these discussions is the traditional, nuclear household. Yet, as we have read, meaningful, long-term, mutually supportive, interpersonal relationships also occur within non-nuclear family households. Such relationships exist even beyond extended family households to include "intentional households", allowing people in shared residences to act on those "family values", as Pollak writes. Through the variety of shared housing options, households have more ways to stay together through changing household structures and situations, keeping alive their ties to meaningful places, communities, and relationships. The availability of these options and the viability of shared housing correspond: for example, Marris points out that more shared housing available means more opportunities to link desirable co-residents and agreeable social contracts in the shared living situation. Providing a variety of options, however, requires greater facilitating and funding of shared housing development. This relies on change in societal values so that "new" forms of households will become valid bases for rethinking what housing options are appropriate, or desirable, in our communities.

Although values change as a result of experience, they can also be confronted directly, primarily through education. Without making a moral argument of the kind that is used to support open housing, for example, where the underlying problem of racism is clearly established, it is possible to provide information that can counter the misunderstandings people have about shared housing. At the local, community level concern over property value is the most important single issue. Studies of shared housing's impact on neighborhoods do not support the belief that the presence of shared housing reduces an area's desirability and lowers property values. There are not enough such studies. Perhaps because they inspire the most concern, or because they are the most common form of shared housing to come before local regulatory boards, we know more about group homes than other types of shared housing. We need a summary and evaluation of the existing research on shared housing's impact on property values, and we need systematic studies of the full range of types of shared housing. The market for such information is not only the general public media, although it is an important means of reaching the public. It is equally important to prepare the results of this research for public and professional education. For example, the publications of the Urban Land Institute and the Planning Advisory Service publications of the American Planning Association reach professional audiences who need this information for their own education and the education of the people they serve.

Few people are aware of the possibilities of shared housing so there is a need to demonstrate how alternative designs can satisfy basic shelter values. Because the new and rare often frightens and intimidates, an effort must be made to overcome resistance beyond simply informing people of options. Leavitt describes how implementation difficulties kept her award-winning design for shared live-work units from being built; Marris describes how a housing development's design was modified for political reasons. These compromised and failed attempts to match design to demonstrated need do little if anything to clarify the viability of shared housing.

Policy makers and development administrators, like the general public, need education to open their thinking about housing alternatives. As an example of current thinking, consider the full page advertisement that the US Department of Housing and Urban Development placed in the Home section of the Chicago Tribune on April 22, 1994. It read in part,

> We'll give you $1000 to get over your APARTMENT COMPLEX and into a house. IF YOU'VE GOT AN APARTMENT COMPLEX, you've probably got a lot of problems. Cramped spaces. Loud neighbors. Nosey landlords. Rules and restrictions. The cure? Owning your own home. And HUD makes finding the cure easy . . . We'll get you over your apartment complex once and for all.

HUD is legislatively committed to combatting racial and gender discrimination in housing, but they obviously do not have a similar commitment on structure type and tenure discrimination.

The issue of finance for shared housing is directed primarily to government officials and private lending institutions. Housing consumers will look to lenders for information on options to finance shared housing. Currently there is little information and experience among housing lenders on shared housing finance. The lack of experience is reinforced by a lack of leadership on the part of government lending and insuring agencies in providing information and support to lending for nonconventional housing. Most lending for unconventional housing is done through specialized programs and agencies and does not enter mainstream lending institutions and practices.

Finance issues can be separated for two basic clients of shared housing, although the activities of the two client groups overlap. The first client group wants shared housing primarily as a means to improve housing affordability. Since this housing may be subsidized, and is often for households with long term limited income expectations and with little capital, and for persons with special needs, there is a need for:

- capital funds for start up of projects

- long term subsidy funds

- financial management assistance

- acceptance of unconventional mortgage holders, including nonprofit organizations, limited equity cooperatives, mutual housing associations, etc.

The second client group wants shared housing more for social benefits and improved quality of life than for economic reasons. They too have trouble with financing and have need for:

- acceptance of unconventional mortgage holders such as two or more individuals

- availability of mortgage insurance

- tax treatment comparable to owner-occupants of single-family homes.

The needs of the two groups clearly overlap when an unconventional structure, such as cohousing with communal dining and child care facilities, is proposed for low income female headed households. One end of the problem is at the federal government level. The prevailing policies and programs of federal agencies are locked into a very traditional view of housing and real estate investment. At the other end, and influenced by federal agency policy and direction, local lenders resist financing innovative housing arrangements.

Both education and experimentation are needed. Local lenders' concern for long term investment quality is prudent and responsible. However, as in the history of funding housing in racially mixed areas, the federal government can lead the way to new practices, demonstrating that novelty need not be equated with high investment risk.

REGULATION

As Pollak documented, local development regulations significantly inhibit shared housing. We obviously need more research and development on models of alternative codes and revision of existing codes. This may be a more difficult problem than changing attitudes and practices in housing finance. The local zoning hearing is for many Americans their most immediate and meaningful experience of democracy. To use an old expression, this is "where the rubber meets the road" in urban development. Individual citizens speaking from their existing values expect to influence development decisions in ways that protect and advance their interests. Since these citizens are often motivated by financial interests— protecting their house as their principal economic asset—they are very resistant to development proposals that contain novelty. Even efforts at design alternatives that do not threaten the integrity of single-family development run into opposition, such as neo-traditional planning proposals involving only unconventional spatial arrangement of houses and no change in overall density or in the mix of housing types. Local regulations must become more flexible, while at the same time providing assurance of stability for area occupants.

Local codes are affected both by state enabling legislation and by federal policy. It may be useful to attack the problem on the state legislative level. However, since state legislation is largely permissive and typically grants wide discretion to localities, it is likely that in this area, as with many other issues of urban development such as fair housing, the most successful route to influencing local development practices is through the courts. Cases such as the Mount Laurel decision in New Jersey on the provision of affordable housing in the suburbs establish benchmarks for the reform of local codes. In this situation it is less clear that there is a constitutional issue acceptable to the courts. Certainly some groups are being deprived of the opportunity to live as they wish by current practices, but further legal research is needed to determine the feasibility of their approach to reform.

The federal government can influence local development regulations in a variety of ways. They can support research and development on more flexible regulatory codes through research institutions and professional associations, and follow this initiative with widespread publicity. At the other extreme, some federal funds that flow to local communities, such as community development block grants (CDBGs), can require localities to meet certain performance standards. Conceivably, these could include the accommodation of shared housing. Certainly the federal agencies need to take a close look at their own policies and practices to eliminate those which themselves inhibit freedom of housing choice, as well as those which encourage localities and developers to do the same.

DESIGN

People are unlikely to change their conceptions of what constitutes good housing for themselves or their neighbors until they see and experience examples of the new alternatives. There have been some notable experiments and some design competitions on shared housing in this country, but we are still on the bottom of the learning curve. Since many shared housing innovations are only now appearing in this country, we need to study and learn from what others have done. As Ahrentzen describes, experience with shared housing is rich and varied. Much of it is directly translatable to our situation because of basic cultural and value similarities. Yet shared housing experience in very different settings will also be helpful to look at. Through international aid and development agencies many less developed countries have sponsored innovation in affordable housing, some of it shared housing. These experiences may be translatable to our setting, especially for affordable shared housing. With the results of studies of existing shared housing in hand, we need to foster experimentation in design and in development that can be monitored, to learn from experience in our society.

We know little about the demand for shared housing, especially for shared housing choices that are based on life style choices, such as combining home and work space, and sharing dining, child care and other activities. While demand will change as people become more familiar with shared housing, as the population ages and as new household patterns form it is important that we begin to systematically identify and analyze this segment of the housing market. Such information will help developers and local development officials reinforce acceptance of shared housing in the general population.

* * *

The burden of argument in this book is to show how diverse forms of shared housing respond to the needs of particular groups of people, supporting their social and economic efforts to live well, to respond to and recover from crises, to maintain family structure and meaningful social relationships, to help others. The chapters in this book provide evidence and arguments that shared housing does not deserve the stigma of dependence it often evokes among believers in the American dream of one family—one house. There are many kinds of shared housing arrangements and most will not likely depress neighboring property values or violate community values. This variety helps meet the diverse needs of a growing number of people who cannot or do not want to live in the traditional housing now available. Their needs and choices should be honored.

Bibliography

Abramovitz, Mimi. 1988. *Regulating the Lives of Women: Social Welfare Policy from Colonial Times to the Present* (Boston: South End Press).

Ahrentzen, Sherry B. 1987. *Blurring Boundaries: Socio-Spatial Consequences of Working at Home* (Milwaukee, Wisconsin: Center for Architectural and Planning Research, University of Wisconsin-Milwaukee).

Ahrentzen, Sherry B. 1989. "Overview of Housing for Single-Parent Families." In K. Franck and S. Ahrentzen, eds., *New Households, New Housing* (New York: Van Nostrand Reinhold).

Ahrentzen, Sherry B. 1991. *Hybrid Housing* (Milwaukee: Center for Architectural and Planning Research, University of Wisconsin-Milwaukee).

Ahrentzen, Sherry B. 1992. "Home As A Workplace in the Lives of Women" in I. Altman and S. Low, eds., *Place Attachment* (New York: Plenum Press).

Allen, Sheila and Carol Wolkowitz. 1987. *Homeworking: Myths and Realities* (London: Macmillan Education).

Apgar, William C. Jr. 1990. "The Nation's Housing: A Review of Past Trends and Future Prospects for Housing in America". In D. DiPasquale and L. Keyes, eds., *Building Foundations: Housing and Federal Policy* (Philadelphia: University of Pennsylvania Press).

Baer, William C. 1986. "The Shadow Market in Housing." *Scientific American*: 255 (5).

Baran, Barbara. 1988. "Office Automation and Women's Work: the Technological Transformation of the Insurance Industry," in R.E. Pahl, ed., *On Work: Historical, Comparative and Theoretical Approaches* (Oxford: Basil Blackwell).

Barton, Stephen and Carol J. Silverman. 1994. *Common Interest Communities: Private Governments and the Public Interest* (Berkeley: University of California, Institute of Governmental Studies).

Baum, Alice and Donald Burnes. 1993. *A Nation in Denial: The Truth About Homelessness* (Colorado Springs: Westview Press).

Bianchi, Suzanne M. and Daphne Spain. 1986. *American Women in Transition* (New York: Russell Sage Foundation).

Birch, Eugenie, ed. 1985. *The Unsheltered Woman: Women and Housing in the 80s* (New Brunswick, NJ: Center For Urban Policy Research).

Blank, Roberta M. 1988. "Women's Paid Work, Household Income, and Household Well-being," in S. E. Rix, ed., *The American Woman, 1988–89* (New York: W.W. Norton and Company)1.

Bluestone, Barry and Bennett Harrison. 1982. *The Deindustrialization of America: Plant Closings, Community Abandonment, and the Dismantling of Basic Industry* (New York: Basic Books).

Boris, Eileen. 1989. "Black Women and Paid Labor in the Home: Industrial Homework in Chicago in the 1920s," in Eileen Boris and Cynthia R. Daniels, eds., *Homework: Historical and Contemporary Perspectives on Paid Labor at Home* (Urbana: University of Illinois Press).

Burnett, John. (1986 2nd ed.,). *A Social History of Housing: 1815–1985* (London: Methuen).

Burt, Martha. 1992. *Over the Edge: The Growth of Homelessness in the 1980s* (New York: Russell Sage Foundation).

Christopherson, Susan. 1989. "Flexibility in the U.S. Service Economy and the Emerging Spatial Division of Labour." *Trans. Inst. Br. Geogr. N.S.* 14: 131–143.

Community Associations Institute, 1993 *Community Associations Factbook* (Alexandria, VA: Community Associations Institute).

Daniels, Cynthia R. 1989. "Between Home and Factory: Homeworkers and the State," in Eileen Boris and Cynthia R. Daniels, eds., *Homework: Historical and Contemporary Perspectives on Paid Labor at Home* (Urbana: University of Illinois Press).

Dear, Michael and Jennifer Wolch. 1993. *Malign Neglect: Homelessness in an American City* (San Francisco: Jossey-Bass).

Despres, Carole. 1991. *The Form, Experience and Meaning of Home in Shared Housing*. Doctoral dissertation. Dept. of Architecture, University of Wisconsin-Milwaukee.

Devaney, F. John. 1994. *Tracking the American Dream: 50 Years of Housing History from the Census Bureau* (Washington D.C.: U.S. Department of Commerce, Economics and Statistics Administration, Bureau of the Census).

Evans, Sara M. 1989. *Born for Liberty: A History of Women in America* (New York: The Free Press).

Feagin, Joe R. and Michael Peter Smith, eds. 1987. *The Capitalist City: Global Restructuring and Community Politics* (Oxford: Basil Blackwell).

Fernandez-Kelly, M. Patricia and Anna M. Garcia. 1989. "Hispanic Women and Homework: Women in the Informal Economy of Miami and Los Angeles," in Eileen Boris and Cynthia R. Daniels, eds., *Homework: Historical and Contemporary Perspectives on Paid Labor at Home* (Urbana: University of Illinois Press).

Finch, Janet and Dulcie Groves, eds. 1983. *A Labour of Love: Women, Work and Caring* (London: Routledge and Kegan Paul).

Franck, Karen A. 1989. "Overview of Collective and Shared Housing," in Karen A. Franck and Sherry Ahrentzen, eds., *New Households, New Housing* (New York: Van Nostrand Reinhold).

Franck, Karen A. and Sherry Ahrentzen, eds. 1989. *New Households, New Housing* (New York: Van Nostrand Reinhold).

Garber, Wendy. 1991. *Housing Ideals and Disappointments: A Socio-Architectural Study of Alternative Housing for Women*. Masters thesis. Dept. of Architecture, University of Wisconsin-Milwaukee.

Garfinkel, Harold. 1967. *Studies in Ethnomethodology* (New York: Prentice-Hall).

Gatlin, Rochelle. 1987. *American Women Since 1945* (Jackson, Mississippi: University Press of Mississippi).

Gellen, Martin. 1985. *Accessory Apartments in Single-Family Houses* (New Brunswick, NJ: Transaction Books).

Goodchild, Barry. 1991. "Postmodernism and Housing: A Guide to Design Theory." *Housing Studies* 6:131–144.

Gordon, Jacques. 1987. *Hidden Housing Production: Residential Conversion Activity in the City of Boston*. Doctoral dissertation. Department of Urban Studies and Planning, Massachusetts Institute of Technology.

Groth, Paul. 1994. *Living Downtown* (Berkeley: University of California Press).

Gurstein, Penny. 1990. "The Home as Information Factory: The Changing Role of the Home for Home-Based Workers," in Marc M. Angelil, ed., *On Architecture, The City, and Technology* (Stoneham, MA.: Butterworth-Heinemann).

Haber, Sheldon E., Enrique J. Lamas, and Jules H. Lichtenstein. 1987. "On Their Own: The Self-Employed and Others in Private Business." *Monthly Labor Review* :17–23.

Harley, Sharon. 1990. "For the Good of Family and Race: Gender, Work, and Domestic Roles in the Black Community, 1880–1930." *SIGNS*:336–349.

Harvey, David. 1985. *Consciousness and the Urban Experience: Studies in the History and Theory of Capitalist Urbanization* (Baltimore: The Johns Hopkins University Press).

Hayden, Dolores. 1981. *The Grand Domestic Revolution* (Cambridge: M.I.T. Press).

Hayden, Dolores. 1984. *Redesigning the American Dream: The Future of Housing, Work, and Family Life* (New York: W.W. Norton, and Co., Inc.).

Hendershott, P.H. and M.T. Smith. 1988. "Housing Inventory Change and the Role of Existing Structures, 1961–1985." *American Real Estate and Urban Economics Association Journal*: 16 (4), pp. 364–376.

Hertzberger, Herman. 1986. *Recent Works* (Amsterdam: Archis).

Hoch, Charles and Robert Slayton. 1989. *New Homeless and Old: Community and the Skid Row Hotel* (Philadelphia: Temple University Press).

Jackson, Kenneth. 1985. *Crabgrass Frontier: The Suburbanization of the United States* (New York: Oxford Univesity Press).

Keller, Suzanne. 1981. *Building on Women* (Lexington, Massachusetts: Lexington Books).

Kessler-Harris, Alice. 1982. *Out to Work: A History of Wage-Earning Women in the United States* (New York: Oxford University Press).

Leavitt, Jacqueline. 1989. "Two Prototypical Designs for Single Parents: The Congregate House and the New American House," in Karen A. Franck and Sherry Ahrentzen, eds., *New Households, New Housing* (New York: Van Nostrand Reinhold).

Leavitt, Jacqueline. Unpublished manuscript. *The Double Dream: The Single Family House and Community*.

Leavitt, Jacqueline. 1990. "The Architect and the Housewife" (Paper presented at the American Collegiate Schools of Architecture and Technology Conference, Los Angeles).

Leavitt, Jacquiline and Susan Saegert. 1989. *From Abandonment to Hope: The Making of Community Households in Harlem*: (New York: Columbia University Press).

Lefebvre, Henri. trans. 1991. *The Production of Space*, translated by Donald Nicholson-Smith (Cambridge: Basil Blackwell).

Liebow, Elliot. 1993. *Tell Them Who I Am: The Lives of Homeless Women* (New York: The Free Press).

Leidner, Robin. 1988. "Home Work: A Study in the Interaction of Work and Family Organization." *Sociology of Work*: 4:69–94.

Little, Jo, Linda Peake and Pat Richardson. 1988. *Women in Cities: Gender & the Urban Environment* (London: Macmillan).

Lozano, Beverly. 1989. *The Invisible Work Force: Transforming American Business with Outside and Home-Based Workers* (New York: The Free Press).

Lubell, Harold. 1991. *The Informal Sector in the 1980s and 1990s*. Paris: Organisation for Economic Co-operation and Development.

Marcus, Clare Cooper and Wendy Sarkissian. 1986. *Housing as if People Mattered* (Berkeley: University of Calif. Press).

Marris, Peter. 1961. *Family and Social Change in an African City* (London: Routledge and Kegan Paul).

Marris, Peter and Anthony Somerset. 1971. *African Businessmen* (London: Routledge and Kegan Paul).

Matrix. 1984. *Making Space: Women and the Man Made Environment* (London: Pluto Press).

Matthews, Glenna. 1987. *"Just a Housewife": The Rise and Fall of Domesticity in America* (New York: Oxford University Press).

McCamant, Kathryn and Charles Durrett. 1988. *Cohousing: A Contemporary Approach to Housing Ourselves* (Berkeley: Habitat Press/Ten Speed Press).

McClain, Janet with Cassie Doyle. 1984. *Women and Housing: Changing Needs and the Failure of Policy* (Ottawa: James Lorimer and Company).

McKenzie, Evan. 1994. *Privatopia: Homeowner Associations and the Rise of Residential Private Government* (New Haven and London: Yale University Press).

Morgenstern, Oscar. 1963. *On the Accuracy of Economic Observations*, 2nd edition. New York: Oxford University Press.

Moser, Caroline O.N. and Linda Peake. 1987. *Women, Human Settlements, and Housing* (London: Tavistock Publications).

Nielsen, Lise Drewes. 1991. "Flexibility, Gender and Local Labour Markets—Some Examples from Denmark." *International Journal of Urban and Regional Research*: 15:42–54.

Pahl, R.E., ed. 1988. *On Work: Historical, Comparative and Theoretical Approaches* (Oxford: Basil Blackwell).

Peattie, Lisa. 1987. "An Idea in Good Currency and How It Grew: The Informal Sector". In *World Development*: 15:851–860.

Pickvance, C.G. 1976. *Urban Sociology: Critical Essays* (New York: St. Martin's Press).

Pollak, Patricia B. 1991. "Zoning Matters in a Kinder Gentler Nation: Balancing Needs, Rights and Political Realities for Shared Residences for the Elderly" in St. Louis University *Public Law Review*: Vol. X, No. 2.

Pratt, Geraldine and Susan Hanson. 1991. "On the Links Between Home and Work: Family-Household Strategies in a Buoyant Labour Market." *International Journal of Urban and Regional Research*: 15:55–74.

Ringheim, Karen. 1990. *At Risk of Homelessness: The Roles of Income and Rent* (New York: Praeger).

Ritzdorf, Marsha. 1986. "Women and the city: Land use and zoning issues." *Journal of Urban Resources*: 3:23–27.

Rix, Sara E., ed. 1988. *The American Woman 1988–89: A Status Report* (New York: W.W. Norton & Company).

Roberts, Marion. 1991. *Living in a Man-Made World: Gender Assumptions in Modern Housing Designs* (London: Routledge).

Roldan, Martha. 1985. "Industrial Outworking, Struggles for the Reproduction of Working-class Families and Gender Subordination," in Nanneke Redclift and Enzo Mingione, eds. *Beyond Employment: Household, Gender and Subsistence* (Oxford: Basil Blackwell).

Rossi, Peter. 1989. *Down and Out in America: The Origins of Homelessness* (Chicago: University of Chicago Press).

Rubery, Jill, ed. 1988. *Women and Recession* (London: Routledge and Kegan Paul).

Sagalyn, Lynne B. 1982. "Who Owns Rental Housing? Ownership Patterns and Investment Incentives in the Boston Metropolitan Area." Paper presented at a conference sponsored by the Joint Center for Urban Studies of MIT and Harvard University and the Lincoln Institute for Land Policy, July.

Scharf, Lois. 1980. *To Work and To Wed: Female Employment, Feminism, and the Great Depression* (Westport, Connecticut: Greenwood Press).

Sheine and Leavitt. 1991. Scenarios presented on board presentation for *Progressive Architecture* competition.

Soja, Edward. 1989. *Postmodern Geographies: The Reassertion of Space in Critical Social Theory* (London: Verso).

Sprague, Joan Forrester. 1991. *More Than Housing: Lifeboats for Women and Children* (Boston: Butterworth Architecture).

Stoner, Jill. 1989. "The Party Wall as the Architecture of Sharing," in Karen A. Franck and Sherry B. Ahrentzen, eds. *New Households, New Housing* (New York: Van Nostrand Reinhold).

Strassmann, W. Paul. 1985. "Home Based Restaurants, Snack Bars, and Retail Stores: Their Contribution to Income and Employment in Lima, Peru," (Michigan State University, Working Paper #86).

Thiberg, Sven, ed. 1990, tr. *Housing Research and Design in Sweden* (Stockholm: Swedish Council for Building Research).

Toffler, Alvin. 1980. *The Third Wave* (New York: Morrow).

U.S. Bureau of the Census. 1991. *Census of Housing, 1973–83 Components of Inventory Change*. Washington, D.C.: Government Printing Office.

Venti, Steven F. and David A. Wise. 1989. "Aging, Moving and Housing Wealth," in D. Wise ed., *The Economics of Aging* (Chicago: University of Chicago Press).

Wekerle, Gerda, and Rebecca Peterson, and David Morley. 1980. *New Space for Women* (Boulder, Co.: Westview Press).

Wekerle, Gerda R. and Brent Rutherford. 1989. "The Mobility of Capital and the Immobility of Female Labor: Responses to Economic Restructuring," in Jennifer Wolch and Michael Dear, eds., *The Power of Geography: How Territory Shapes Social Life* (Boston: Unwin Hyman).

Women's City Club. 1920. "Tenement Home Work in New York City." (New York: Women's City Club of New York).

Wright, Gwendolyn. 1981. *Building the Dream: A Social History of Housing in America* (New York: Pantheon Books).

Wright, James. 1989. *Address Unknown: The Homeless in America* (New York: Aldine de Gruyter).

Contributors

Sherry Ahrentzen, Associate Professor of Architecture at the University of Wisconsin-Milwaukee, has published articles on new forms of housing for diverse types of non-traditional households and uses, in journals such as *Environment and Behavior* and *Journal of Architectural and Planning Research*. She has received several grants for her research in this area, notably from the National Endowment for the Arts and the National Science Foundation; one resulting in the report *Hybrid Housing* (1991). In 1989, she and Karen A. Franck co-edited the book *New Households, New Housing*.

Jean Butzen serves as Executive Director of Lakefront SRO Corporation in Chicago, Illinois.

Richard J. Biddlecombe is the General Secretary of Abbeyfield International and the volunteer Chairman of The Abbeyfield Potters Bar and District Society which owns and manages two supportive houses, currently being upgraded to "Extended Care" standards. He has a wide experience of Abbeyfield at International, National and local levels and by invitation has spoken on the work of the charity in Spain and the USA and to numerous groups in the UK. Through Abbeyfield International he is regularly in touch with existing and potential Abbeyfielders and other interested parties from all corners of the world.

Jana Carp is a doctoral student in Public Policy Analysis at the University of Illinois at Chicago; her research interests involve culturally-specific uses of contemporary American public and common places, public art, and planning theory. She wrote portions of The Image Bank for Teaching World Religions, sponsored by the National Endowment for the Humanities.

Anna Hardman is an urban planner and economist who received her B.A. in Philosophy, Politics and Economics from Oxford University and

147

her masters degree and Ph.D. in urban planning from the Massachusetts Institute of Technology. She is currently Assistant Professor of Economics and Urban Planning at Virginia Polytechnic Institute and State University. Her research focuses on urban housing markets, the impacts of regulation on housing supply and the market impacts when those regulations are evaded.

George Hemmens is Professor in the College of Urban Planning and Public Affairs, and Co-Director of the City Design Center in the College of Architecture and the Arts at the University of Illinois at Chicago.

Charles Hoch is Associate Professor, College of Urban Planning and Public Affairs at the University of Illinois at Chicago. He is the author of *What Planners Do: Power, Politics and Persuasion* (Planner's Press, 1994) and co-author of *New Homeless and Old: Community and the Skid Row Hotel* (Temple University Press, 1989).

Jacqueline Leavitt is Associate Professor in the Urban Planning Program at the University of California, Los Angeles. She co-authored The *Community Household* (Columbia University Press, 1989) with Susan Saegert.

Peter Marris is a professor emeritus of the University of California, Los Angeles, and presently teaching at Yale. He is the author, among other books, of *Loss and Change*, and *Meaning and Action*, and a forthcoming work on the management of uncertainty.

Patricia Baron Pollak is Associate Professor, Department of Consumer Economics and Housing at Cornell University, in the NYS College of Human Ecology at Cornell University. She is author of *Key Issues for Shared Residences for Older Persons* (American Association of Retired Persons, 1991), and numerous articles on housing and zoning.

Index

149